MONETISING THE EMPLOYEE EXPERIENCE

PRAISE FOR MONETISING THE EMPLOYEE EXPERIENCE

"As many companies move into a hybrid workforce model, having effective EX strategies to really inspire and motivate your people seems more important than ever. The book clearly creates the case and provides practical tools on the 'how' to help you to achieve this."

ALYSON TAYLOR, FORMER HEAD OF PEOPLE, KPMG (KUWAIT)

"We spend huge amounts of time and resources creating the best Customer Experience. As *Monetising the Employee Experience* shows, we're missing a trick. This book makes a powerful business case for investing in the EX, and gives you the information and tools to create an effective EX. 10/10 would recommend."

PETER VAN DER MERWE, HEAD OF STRATEGY AND CONTENT, BYDESIGN COMMUNICATIONS

"Every now and then a book comes along that joins the dots up. This book does this so eloquently and with ease. With most books focussing on either 'Employee Experience' or 'Customer Experience' it's great to read a book that addresses both and links them in a succinct and pragmatic way. Behind all great organisations lie great people, so it follows that great employee experiences leads to great products/services and satisfied clients.

"This book clearly and expertly outlines the importance of investing in EX, supports you in delivering the business case, and then gives you the tools to act. A must-read to enable you to create effective and productive teams that achieve goals and exceed targets."

STEVE JONES, FOUNDER, SKILLS FOR BUSINESS

"This book is bang up-to-date, bang up-to-relevant-and-researched, and bang up-to-being a real game changer for organisations looking for a serious and sustainable competitive advantage. Indeed, I think all organisations who read it and act on its advice are going to power ahead over the next decade; those who simply carry on as usual will be in jeopardy of failure or—possibly worse—in perpetual need of bail-outs to extend their existential misery. So, get on board, get reading, and get on with acting out the wisdom and insights brimming throughout this important contribution to organisational development.

"The central contention of the book is that the employee experience is equally if not more important than the customer experience; the latter depends on the former, in fact. Furthermore, the authors demonstrate conclusively that the ROI of our business is significantly increased once we adopt this line of thinking and this level of methodology. One of the most pleasing aspects of this book is the foregrounding of staff productivity and how to really impact this. Surely, if there was even the faintest chance that we could meaningfully increase productivity, then we would embrace it with every muscle and sinew in our body! This book shows you exactly how to do it; truly, it is ground-breaking. I cannot recommend it enough."
JAMES SALE, AUTHOR, MAPPING MOTIVATION

"To transform your business and bottom line, it's time to rewrite the role for your CEO—here's celebrating the birth of the Chief Experience Officer."
FIONA ANDERSON, FOUNDER, MY CHANGE EXPERT AND VALUINGYOU

MONETISING THE EMPLOYEE EXPERIENCE

How to prove the ROI for investing in your people and unlock lost productivity

MIKE SHARPLES and NICHOLAS WARDLE

Milestone House
219 Winchester Road
Chandlers Ford
Hampshire
SO53 2DX
United Kingdom

ISBN: 978-1-5272-8686-3

Printed and bound in Great Britain by KDP.
Cover art and design, and interior figures by Nick Dale.

www.exopportunity.com

CONTENTS

ABOUT THE AUTHORS

MIKE SHARPLES

Mike is an experienced business leader and entrepreneur, with a varied career spanning over 35 years, the last 25 of which have been spent running businesses in MD & CEO roles. Mike started his career at the tender age of 17, joining a successful US computer manufacturer and at 21 he became the youngest business unit manager globally with responsibility for customers across the EMEA region. He set up his first business in 1994, helping businesses in London benefit from the advances in PC and thin client technology, eventually focusing on software and the development of some of the first web-based intranets and portals. Over the years his clients have included global technology giants such as IBM and Cisco, as well as FTSE100 companies such as Associated British Foods and BAA, and charities like the Royal British Legion. Mike now dedicates his time to improving the lives of employees at work, as CEO and Head of Strategy at Brand Experiences.

NICHOLAS WARDLE

Nicholas is an award-winning employee experience practitioner with over 15 years' experience in the employee experience/comms/engagement space, both in the UK and in the Middle East. He has worked across many sectors, including the arts, television, local government, retail and housing. Nicholas is a Fellow of the Institute of Internal Communications (IoIC), and a committee member of both Engage for Success, and IoIC London. His mantra is to 'keep the complex, simple' and he believes that the employee experience should have parity with the customer experience.

ACKNOWLEDGEMENTS

There used to be a cliché about business plans being made down the pub on the back of a cigarette packet. The origins of this book came about in the same kind of venue, but more modern technology was used to sketch the initial plans.

In his role as a practitioner, Nicholas was a client of Mike's organisation, Brand Experiences. We met in a pub after work one day to check in on the progress of deliverables for a business change campaign. Nicholas was feeling a little frustrated as he'd been to yet another internal comms/employee engagement event which promised much, but delivered nothing new. The talk was on reaching the frontline, the sell was 'we can show you how'. The 'how' was never mentioned, perhaps because you had to buy-in the expertise later to find out, or maybe the speakers thought simply discussing some survey results on this well-trodden topic was enough to send people away satisfied. Nicholas wanted to offer 'something' practical to his industry, and to employees in general, which would help to enrich their working lives.

Mike understood this. Having spent decades in boardrooms he knew that the focus was almost always on the customer. Whereas money would be willingly given to chase new prospects or to keep customers happy, very little, if anything, was set aside to spend on employees, other than salaries and on-costs (pensions etc.). So, with such little buy-in from senior leaders for the employee experience, it was no wonder that the industry was floundering, and employees were being sold short.

Mike also had personal reasons for desiring that the welfare and esteem of employees was highlighted; hence, came the seeds for this book and a support package called The Employee Experience Opportunity (EXO), which we later partnered with the Institute of Internal Communications (IoIC) on. The support and input from Jennifer Sproul, Chief Executive of the IoIC and her team has proven invaluable—both on the EXO and the writing of this book.

We would both like to thank Joseph Sale for his editorial guidance on this book. His enthusiasm for the topic and his counsel on shaping and editing the content is really appreciated. We would also both like to thank Nick Dale for his input on the design and for producing almost all of the graphics that you see in this book. As well as being a first-class graphic designer and videographer, Nick also has the firmest handshake in the business.

Mike would like to thank his wife, Jacqui and four children; Mica, Paige, Jake and Luke for their continued support and inspiration to make a difference. He is also thankful for his colleagues at Brand Experiences for their dedication to turning his vision into a reality. And, finally, is grateful for the chance meeting (in a car park, of all places) with Steve Jones that ultimately led to partnering with him on the creation of mojo, the employee motivation and productivity platform for business.

Nicholas would like to thank his family for their support, and his fellow volunteers at Engage for Success and the Institute of Internal Communication for being a constant source of inspiration.

FOREWORD

BY **JENNIFER SPROUL,** CHIEF EXECUTIVE,
INSTITUTE OF INTERNAL COMMUNICATION

As the Chief Executive of the Institute of Internal Communication I am passionate about driving our message that people drive the success of organisations, so it is vital to communicate with them effectively. Employees deserve to feel that they matter, and that they are valued, kept informed, connected, and given a sense of purpose through authentic and high standard experiences.

I remember sitting down with Mike and Nicholas (who is a Fellow of the IoIC) back in 2019, sharing our aligned passion to drive employee experience further up the agenda in organisations and give it parity to customer experience. And in these conversations how could we support and empower our community of internal communication professionals to drive the Employee Experience Opportunity. It was clear from Mike and Nicholas's passion that they wanted to do this by creating discussion, insight, and finally practical solutions to empower our community.

When considering employee experience, communication is a constant thread that binds what we say and what we do in organisations. But creating great employee experiences requires collaboration and buy-in amongst key functions and stakeholders; this book is packed with tools and techniques to bring all the key elements together to make the all-important business case and ROI calculation.

Employees are the greatest asset in an organisation. We need to invest in their needs, motivations, and experiences to create organisations that engender an environment which allows them to thrive and feel equally as valued as customers. An organisation that invests in employee experience can achieve greater productivity, innovation, reputation, talent attraction and retention. But more so as we face continued change and transformation in how we work, re-imagining the employee experience is central to creating high-performing organisations. We have an opportunity and with the support of this book we can secure that investment, as not only will it drive organisational results, it will also create a better society overall.

I am grateful to Mike and Nicholas for inviting myself and the IoIC to support their work in driving the Employee Experience Opportunity, to align our shared visions and provide practical support and tools which enables us to make the case to our leadership which shows the tangible impact this will have on our organisations and our people.

THE EMPLOYEE EXPERIENCE OPPORTUNITY

According to 2018 Gallup figures[1], only 15% of employees worldwide feel engaged in their work, leading to the global costs of unproductivity at a staggering $7 trillion. We felt something had to change and wanted to be a part of that change. So, in 2019, we created the Employee Experience Opportunity (EXO), with our strapline being that: We are on a mission to give employee experience parity with customer experience.

We called this project the EXO for several reasons. The headline-grabber is the impact EX can have on the ROI, and we wanted to give people the tools to create their own EX. What we also wanted was for people to recognise the opportunity to stand up and grab the EXO for their organisation and themselves—not necessarily to wait for their HR team to begin, as you may be waiting some time!

In order to kick-start this mission, we approached Jennifer Sproul, Chief Executive of the Institute of Internal Communication (IoIC), to see if they'd like to partner with us. Jennifer was already independently thinking about how EX fits in with Internal Communications, and so agreed. Together, we devised the following.

THE FOUR STAGES OF THE EX ROADMAP

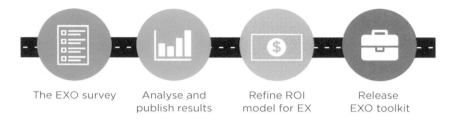

The EXO survey | Analyse and publish results | Refine ROI model for EX | Release EXO toolkit

THE EXO SURVEY

In November 2019 we launched a survey, which included 37 questions related to EX. Around 2,000 people were surveyed. We wanted some original EX research, as any good campaign is evidence-based.

ANALYSE AND PUBLISH THE RESULTS

The survey was due to close in February 2020, but we extended the deadline to August 2020 and added eight further questions related to the impact of Coronavirus. (We felt it would be odd to ignore this rather large modern elephant.) The results are discussed in detail in Section Two.

REFINE ROI MODEL FOR EX

While the survey was open, we finalised our EXOpportunity Calculator™ which you can read about in Section Four. Our desire is for EX practitioners to use this model in relation to their own organisation and show senior leaders the evidence of why it's not 'can they afford to invest in EX?', but 'can they afford not to?'.

RELEASE EXO TOOLKIT

The toolkit is discussed in this book, and downloads to help you to create a compelling EX are available—see Section Seven. For even more on the EXO, visit www.exopportunity.com.

WHO IS THIS BOOK FOR?

Ultimately, we'd like to see this book in the hands of Chief Execs, Chief Operating Officers and as we talk about ROI, Chief Finance Officers. After all, a major aim of ours is to inform decision makers about the EXO and that effective EX increases productivity, which directly impacts upon the bottom line. To throw a stat in early, Gallup[2] find that business units in the top quartile of their global employee engagement database are 17% more productive and 21% more profitable than those in the bottom quartile. We believe that engagement is an output of an effective EX.

We do recognise, however, that this is a busy world in which many are advocating for, and selling, their 'solution' to the problem of disengaged employees and abysmal bottom line. There's a lot of competition to be 'the next book' and ours is not the only one that has likely been thrust into your hands. We intend to show you why our methods and philosophy is something of a trump card.

As this is also a practical 'how to' guide, it's definitely for those responsible for, or those considering being responsible for, EX. Presently, this is usually HR Directors and HR Heads of; although given the appalling low engagement rate at work across the globe, it's apparent that many HR leaders still need to be sold on the importance of EX and how to achieve a great one.

It's possible that anyone—not just HR—could own EX, so we also think this book will be of interest to Internal Communications/Employee Engagement and L&D professionals. You could use this book to bring about an evolution at your organisation!

And, of course, anyone already working in the EX space may benefit from this book. According to Deloitte[3] only 22% of Executives believe that their organisation is building a differentiated EX, so there's plenty of work to be done.

We firmly believe in managing upwards, so would cheer any employee who uses this book to challenge their leaders on why they're not receiving at least a good EX, when it's fairly straightforward to achieve, as we will make clear.

HOW TO USE THIS BOOK

For fans of Simon Sinek, we do explain the why, but we also give the how! Our aim is to give you the means to take action. What we don't do is give pages and pages of anecdotes, case studies or allegorical stories. It's our belief that what we outline will either make sense, or it won't.

We know that Rome wasn't built in a day, and nor can an effective EX. We outline in this book where we think you should begin. We see productivity and culture as the key pillars of an effective EX, and recommend starting with productivity, as it's easier to improve upon and achieve swifter results. We do discuss culture in this book, but more in terms of what it is and isn't, rather than the steps on how to create a great one. This may well come from us later! The scope of this book is to focus on helping you to get your business case delivered, then get you up-and-running using our EXO Toolkit.

Section One is a bit like an Executive Summary. It outlines why EX is integral to business success, why it's as important as CX, and introduces elements of EX you should really focus upon.

As the case for EX clearly hasn't been made yet, in Section Two, we'll help you to do this at your organisation. Using the evidence base of our survey, and other research, we look at the EX state of play, what happens if you ignore EX, where to start your EX improvement journey, and introduce the all-important ROI.

Key to an effective EX is productivity. So, in Section Three, we'll show you how to link this to the ROI, introduce the '3 Es' of Productivity, discuss the link between motivation and productivity, and tell you about a tool we're sure will increase productivity at your organisation.

In Section Four, we flesh out the details of the ROI. We appreciate it may feel like quite some shift moving from soft metrics—such as clicks/views, attendees etc.—to hard metrics such as ROI, but it's really not that difficult; especially as we're going to give you a tool to use to calculate the ROI of EX at your organisation.

In Section Five, we outline all the tools you need to create an effective EX. This includes tools such as Employee Journey Maps, Persona Definitions and Business Case Canvasses.

We do a bit of crystal ball gazing in Section Six, and give some thoughts on who should own EX, why CEOs should up their game, and the impact EX can have on innovation and performance.

And in Section Seven, we give worked examples of EX tools so you can see them in action to give you the confidence to use them. You can download the templates from www.brandexperiences.com/exotoolkit.

By the end of this book, you will understand how EX impacts upon the bottom line, and how it differentiates in retention, talent attraction, productivity, and engagement. And by using the toolkits, you'll be able to create a compelling EX yourself. Not bad, eh?

INTRODUCTION

To use familiar business terminology, this introduction is rather like an Exec Summary. We want to get straight to the point and outline up front why your organisation needs to invest in EX. So, according to Perkbox[1] research, an excellent EX leads to:

- 2.3x greater revenue growth
- 5x better shareholder return
- 21% higher profitability
- 17% higher productivity
- 10% increase in customer ratings

With stats like these, it's a wonder why EX isn't a top three priority for every CEO. But it clearly isn't as worldwide productivity and engagement levels are so low. This is despite this statement coming from the mouths of almost every CEO:

"Our employees are our best asset"

The evidence points to there clearly being a say-do gap. Your EX shouldn't be ignored as it can offer a compelling ROI, which benefits everyone: customers, employees and stakeholders. Ask yourself:

- How much does your organisation spend on attracting new customers and attempting to keep current ones happy versus attracting new talent and keeping employees happy?
- How much does your organisation spend on tech and tools to support an effective CX versus how much is spent on an effective EX?
- How many employees do you have designing and improving touchpoints on the customer journey versus how many employees do you have designing and improving touchpoints on the employee journey?

EX IS UNDERVALUED AND UNDERFUNDED

Only those who aren't on LinkedIn will have missed Richard Branson's quote: *Clients do not come first. Employees come first. If you take care of your employees, they will take care of your clients.* The customer may well be king, but the king will soon look for different subjects if served with indifference. It's baffling that many senior leaders seem to expect their employees to offer an exceptional customer service, while offering them an exceptionally poor one.

EX has a more compelling ROI than CX. Yes, you read that right. It's easier to obtain, quicker to realise, and potentially more valuable. If an organisation of 1,000 employees has an annual revenue of £220M, and a sales campaign yielded £1M, then this would be widely celebrated. As we will show you later in this book, if the same organisation improved the motivation of its employees by just 5%, they can improve lost productivity by £1.6M—and that's every year on an ongoing basis. EX is a gift that keeps on giving, unlike gambling on sales campaigns. And retained, motivated employees are likely to contribute to sales. So why don't all senior leaders recognise this?

Remarkably, given its broad reach, EX is not just often considered a poor relation to CX, but also to some internal functions. For example, IT has made the case for investing in tech and therefore money is readily dished out for new tools and pieces of equipment. Governance has made the case for investing in fail safe data processes and receives good levels of funding towards this end. Have you ever heard of someone 'doing Governance' as an add-on? No, so why are many EX activities performed by HR employees as an add-on to their duties?

From our experience, in most organisations, EX just happens. It's a collection of siloed touchpoints owned by different people, each reflecting the personality of that person. It's rare that we find an organisation that has an EX strategy, let alone defined Employee Journey Maps, Empathy Maps and Employee Lifecycles. To fully drive this point home, imagine if you let your CX just 'happen'? The outcome would be disastrous—the same goes for EX.

PANDEMICS AND THE REIMAGINED WORKPLACE

There have been tens of surveys on the impact of Covid-19 on the workplace. Our research shows that only a third of respondents want to go back to working how they were before offices were locked down. This is in-line with other surveys we have seen.

For years, organisations have talked about the importance of a work/life balance, without taking many steps towards achieving it. As a result of Covid-19, the working from home genie is firmly out of the bottle and it seems certain that moving forward, home-working will become more common place. *Why can't I work from home?* is being replaced with *Why should I come into the office?* And, certainly, bulk perks such as free fruit in the office will no longer have the same impact.

Often out of the darkness comes the light, and there has been some positive working outcomes from the pandemic. With the rise in Microsoft Teams or Zoom calls, colleagues are viewing each other more as human beings as you get to take a peek into their private lives. Possibly because of this, and a requirement for line managers to check in more often with their teams, some organisations have seen a positive improvement in their engagement levels. A consequence of this, though, is that people are increasingly expecting to be treated as individuals and these 'internal customers' will want more of a personalised EX. So, it will need to be designed with this in mind.

An awful consequence of Covid-19 is that many organisations are culling jobs. This means a focus is required on more for less. As we will come onto later on it's easier to 'shift the needle' with EX than CX. Think of it this way—those forced into lockdown during Covid-19—all of a sudden had to get creative with cooking, with limited access to shops. With seemingly little effort, families began producing wonderful meals with ingredients left in cupboards, which were just—if not more—nutritional than ready meals. They created more with less, with often very tasty results. There's a metaphor there: making the best out of what you already have is an easier route to success than chasing something new. And, if you achieve employee involvement and participation at your organisation, then the chances are that the abysmal 15% employee engagement rate across the world will start to rise. Only by seeking to utilise the strengths of your employees can you begin on the ladder to achieve the high-performing culture which many organisations talk about but so few achieve.

With a rise in homeworking, the old-fashioned productivity via presenteeism will be more difficult to achieve—not that we subscribe to this form of management. Therefore, many organisations are going to have to use new methods to try to achieve these rises. It's our belief that you can achieve such rises by focusing on the three Es of productivity: Energy/Empathy/Environment. All of these are part of an effective EX and will be discussed in more detail in Section Three.

Our research tells us that 97% of people believe that EX has an impact upon productivity, and the evidence is there at the start of this section to show the positive results. (There's more evidence to come in Section Two where we make the case for EX.) Much as customers desire a positive experience, so do employees. A major issue is that many of those responsible for EX simply don't have the grasp of the topic. It's not an extension of an HR Business Partner role, it's a new set of skills and tools entirely.

EX is about putting people at the heart of every organisation, because everyone matters at work. Effective EX leads to a more motivated, engaged and productive workforce—which will, ultimately, lead to a positive impact upon the bottom line.

WHY YOU NEED THE EX FACTOR

IN THIS SECTION WE DISCUSS:

What EX is

That EX and CX are two sides of the same coin

How it should be easier to increase the ROI on EX than CX

The touchpoints on the Employee Journey Map

The importance of the war for talent

The importance of the war to retain talent

OUR DEFINITION OF EX

Everything of importance has a definition and we define EX as:

Short version:

> *"The entire relationship between employee and employer. It encompasses every interaction and touchpoint at every stage of the Employee Lifecycle."*

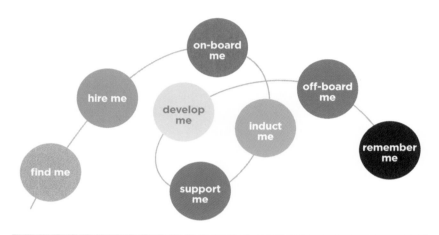

THE EMPLOYEE LIFECYCLE

Long version:

> *"The entire relationship between employee and employer, including: how the employer treats their employees, how the relationship evolves, the work environment, the culture both parties operate in, and the tools provided to get the job done. It encompasses every interaction and touchpoint with the organisation and its stakeholders at every stage of the Employee Lifecycle."*

In short, it's how you treat your employees. So, it's the relationships and how these are handled; the work environment and if this is conducive to productive work; the culture; and the technology and tools to enable people to do their job well. Employee engagement, morale, and productivity are all outcomes of a good EX.

If people have a good or great EX, it stands to reason that they'll be happy or very happy at work. Clap-happy as this sounds, usually happy hands are busy hands! We agree with the sentiments from the *wethrive*[5] *Future of Employee Engagement Report 2019*:

'It makes perfect sense that if you work with a good group of people who have the same aims, have the resources you need to work well, feel competent in your job, and are acknowledged for the work you do, you will be much more likely to go in to work with a smile and work enthusiastically than if the conditions and culture make working life unpleasant.'

EX AND CX ARE TWO SIDES OF THE SAME COIN

CX is a fairly well to very well-established term in business these days. It's true that the quality of customer service ranges wildly, so not everyone has got it right, but most organisations of size will dedicate time and resources to creating things to help to improve CX such as Customer Journey Maps and Customer Personas, and will spend millions on tools such as Customer Contact Management systems and Customer Relationship Management systems.

It's generally understood that improvements in CX lead to better organisational performance. Recent success stories, such as Airbnb and Netflix, have differentiated themselves through their CX and it's this that's given them the competitive advantage.

That's all well and good, but, if it works for CX, why not for EX? As we keep asking, does your organisation have Employee Journey Maps and Employee Personas? It would be of no surprise to us if it doesn't, because our research shows that 53% either strongly agree or agree that their organisation values customers more than its employees. Yet given the importance of customers, it's baffling that only 49% strongly agree or agree that their organisation keeps them up-to-date with what their customers say about them. There's a disconnect here.

THE BRAND EXPERIENCES MAP

Our experience has been that whereas senior leaders see the benefit of spending money to attract and retain customers, they're less keen on spending money on attracting and retaining employees. Lots of money is spent on freebie extras for new customers; are you offering your newly hired talent a series of sweeteners as they join?

Respondents to the 2020 Edelman Trust Barometer[6] ranked the following groups in order of importance to a company achieving long-term success: Customers 38%, Employees 37%, Shareholders 13%, Communities 12%. Almost neck and neck between EX and CX!

Similarly, we see Employee Experience and Customer Experience as two intertwined tree roots: one root is often watered and given attention, whereas the other is left to dry-out; and you need both to make a strong and stable tree! Your data people probably talk about 'data being the new gold' and highlight the importance of good quality data. 'Rubbish in, rubbish out' has become a catchphrase. The same is true of your 'brand experience'—which is the outcome of EX and CX. If you hire rubbish people and give them a rubbish experience, then they'll provide a rubbish service to your customers. We look at it like EX x CX = BX^2. In other words, get both right, and you'll offer the best possible brand experience.

We agree with what Denise Lee Yohn says in her book *Fusion*[7] that you should 'directly and explicitly integrate your CX with your EX'. Systems and processes should be designed with the customer **and** employees in mind, and it helps if those responsible for creating the experiences know, understand, and respect the frontline. As CX is more mature than EX, those focusing on the latter can use established tools and methodologies that are successful for the former. There really is no need to do too much reinventing of the wheel. In Section Six, we talk more about integrating EX and CX, and in Section Seven, we point you to some tools to help to create great employee experiences.

HOW IT SHOULD BE EASIER TO ACHIEVE ROI ON EX THAN CX

Focusing on improving your CX is a waste of time, unless you have the EX bit right first. It's easier to improve your EX as you already have your captive audience: your employees. Investment in CX is gambling on attracting new customers and keeping current ones happy. You may or may not obtain new customers and current ones can shop elsewhere, but you will definitely have your employees every day.

Employees *choose* to work at an organisation. In most cases, there are alternatives available, so something has made them decide to work at yours. It could be the location, the salary, a bigger role, growth plans... whatever it is, they're at one organisation and not another for at least one reason. With some rare exceptions, people come to work with the hope of doing a good job and fulfilling their duties. People become unmotivated and obstructive because of a poor EX; few join an organisation with the intention of behaving this way.

Furthermore, the salaries of your employees are on the profit and loss each month and are likely to be one of your biggest costs. It makes sense to seek to gain maximum effectiveness from this large fixed cost.

As we've stated before, a major reason why we believe that EX should have parity with

CX is that an increase in the quality of EX can directly impact the bottom line. How? Largely through productivity gains. Just imagine how much more profitable your organisation would be if, on average, all employees were 5% more productive? If calls were answered 5% quicker, if the first-time resolution rate rose by 5%, if the quality of new-hires improved by 5%. Productivity leads to performance which leads to profits.

Think about it: is it easier for your organisation to attract more customers, or to obtain more productivity from your employees? (Which, in turn, can often lead to more customers, which can lead to more sales.) This is why EX needs to be taken seriously.

Many organisations have roles such as Customer Experience Officer and Customer Success Manager, so would it not be sensible to have roles such as Employee Experience Officer and Employee Success Manager? After all, as we make no apologies for repeating: EX and CX are two sides of the same coin.

THERE ARE SOME WARS GOING ON...

To bring to life how some simple and cost-effective improvements can bring about an increase in the ROI of EX, we shall broadly consider two touchpoints on the Employee Journey map: Talent Attraction and Talent Retention.

THE WAR TO ATTRACT TALENT

Okay, the phrase is rather hyperbolic, but the war for talent is well established, and the candidate experience is a pivotal part of the EX. We've all heard about a skills shortage, and how organisations are needing to up their game to try to attract the best talent. According to our survey, 58% of people see themselves staying no more than three years at their current organisation. To add a bit more beef to the evidence, Gallup[8] say that 63% of employees believe it is 'very likely' or 'somewhat likely' that they could find a job as good as the one they have. Recruitment in itself costs money, and getting it wrong will cost even more money, not just in terms of recruitment fees, but lost time and productivity.

The Employee Journey starts, of course, at the Talent Attraction stage. This is when the talent has its first glimpse at the organisation via the job advert, job description or possibly the Talent Attraction portal. If these three things are appealing, it should encourage someone to flirt more with an organisation; if not, then the journey ends with the click of a button.

And so it goes on with each new stage of the Talent Attraction touchpoint. There are lots of hinge-points where talent can self-select out of the process, so it's important to create successful 'moments that matter' (sometimes called 'moments of truth'). We speak more about these in Section Five, but, in short, these moments need to be identified and worked at to be the best they can possibly be. Examples of moments that matter in Talent Attraction include:

The job description: which should offer real insight into the role, not simply generic information.

The Talent Attraction portal: which should allow people to 'see' what it's really like at the organisation and feature aspects of your culture, display your values, and showcase your people.

The application form: which should be user-friendly; what does it say about your organisation if you ask for a CV and also make people re-type or cut/paste the same information into text boxes?

The interview offer: which should be as flexible as possible on interview dates/times, not simply be fixed times when it suits the organisation.

The interview: which should focus upon making the candidates feel welcomed, offered refreshments on arrival, and showed courtesy such as being thanked for their time etc..

Communication on status: which should be regular, not simply ignoring candidates until they're next called (or not).

The rejection: which should include an offer of feedback to those you decide not to proceed with—remember that they could be a potential customer, or maybe suitable for other roles in the future; and as a human being they're surely worth more than a standard email—or worse—silence if they're rejected.

Post-offer: this stage should involve lots of communication, staying in touch, inviting people to meet their future colleagues before they start, not simply ignoring them between the offer letter and their first day.

It's not always easy to find the right person for a role. However, if you offer a good-to-great candidate experience, including offering all the information a person needs to feel like they have a sense of what working at your organisation is like, then this should aid you in getting more decisions right than wrong.

It's important that your culture shines through on your Talent Attraction portals. This will make your values and behavioural expectations clear and will help a candidate to get a sense of whether the organisation is right for them. It's much better for someone to self-select themselves out of the running, then to waste time interviewing them, or worse, realise after they've been appointed. It's a bit like online dating, really. A good, honest profile, and regular open dialogue, can help woo the right candidate and can also help the wrong candidates understand that you're not for them.

A bit of time and money spent upfront on getting Talent Attraction right, can save an awful lot of time and money later. Poor hires cost in lack of productivity and will eventually cost even more in terms of having to re-hire—not to mention the reputational damage done when bad hires leave negative messages on Glassdoor and other such sites.

THE WAR TO RETAIN TALENT

A more cost-effective and productive battleground than attraction is the war to retain talent. Talent is, of course, relative, and by no means should just mean top talent. It should never be the case that you wait for someone to threaten to leave before you decide just how important they are!

An example

Here's a little made-up story to display our point.

> Meet Samantha. She's a good Internal Communications Manager, earning £50k. She's emotionally invested in the organisation, performs well, and has some growth potential. If you were to give Samantha an overall score out of ten, it would be an eight.
>
> Like everyone, she'd like a bit more money, especially as she has two kids, and wouldn't mind undertaking the Institute of Internal Communications Masters in IC, costing £6k.
>
> But there's no real budget for bespoke L&D courses and double the cost of the living wage increase (around 4%) is as high as any salary increase would go.
>
> So, Samantha gets on LinkedIn, finds a job similar to the one she already has, gets paid £10k more, and will consider self-funding the Masters if her new employer won't pay.

Her original organisation then looks to recruit at the same salary—perhaps even lower—which would score a few budget brownie points. After a three-month search, which overstretches the remaining IC team members as they're a person short, someone is appointed at £50k, who is of similar standard to Samantha, but it takes six months for them to be as productive, continuing to impact upon the current team.

The cost to recruit the new person is 20% of the salary, which is £10k. Knowing Samantha, she would've stayed if her organisation paid for the Masters and £2k extra. Factor in the extra stress and strain on the remaining team members and the decrease in productivity, then surely doing what you could to keep Samantha would have been the wise move? She may have even stayed for the Masters and just £1k extra. Or maybe just for the Masters! And then you would have one happy, motivated employee, who feels valued. And, in effect, have saved yourself some cash.

So, the moral of this little fable is: to cherish your good performers. In most cases it will take a lot less to retain them, than to recruit someone new. And someone new is always a gamble.

You'll have many Samanthas at your organisation. Imagine the savings in the long run if they were all fairly recognised and encouraged to keep being part of the work family? This is both in terms of reducing recruitment time and fees, and maintaining productivity.

Money is a factor in people deciding whether to join/leave an organisation, but it's by no means the only one. In fact, there are potentially nine different reasons that people show up to work. When we look at motivation in Section Four, we will explore this in greater depth.

Some up-front investment will help to secure new and existing talent, save cash on recruitment, maintain morale, and make you more productive. Talent Attraction and Talent Retention are just two examples of why focusing on the ROI of EX is so important. It really can pay even bigger dividends than focussing on the ROI of CX.

We'll discuss how to create effective touchpoints in more detail in Section Five.

TOP THREE TAKEAWAYS

 If your employees are, indeed, your best asset, you should consider assigning people to work on tools such as Employee Journey Maps and Employee Personas to give yourself the best possible chance of designing an effective EX.

 Does your organisation see EX and CX as two sides of the same coin? There are a host of benefits to having these two functions work more closely together.

 When was the last time you reviewed key stages on the Employee Journey such as Talent Attraction or Talent Retention? A little time and money spent really can help you employ the right people and keep your best employees at your organisation—which saves a lot of money in the long run.

MAKING THE CASE FOR EX

IN THIS SECTION WE DISCUSS:

The impact of an effective EX

Barriers to offering a great EX

The EXO survey—original research on EX

The Three Es of Productivity

The importance of a people-first culture

Key cultural indicators

The benefits of being a values-based organisation

The four enablers of Employee Engagement

The importance of a demonstrable ROI of EX

The figure that we keep coming back to is Gallup's statistic that only 15% of employees worldwide feel engaged, leading to the global costs of unproductivity at a staggering $7 trillion. Whereas we believe that many senior leaders struggle to grasp what engagement means, they do fully understand productivity, especially when they can see it in action. This, for us, is at the heart of EX.

Successful EX, including effective onboarding, employee development and management, will lead to increases in:

- Motivation
- Engagement
- Productivity
- Performance
- Job satisfaction
- Willingness to change
- Employee involvement and participation
- ROI per employee
- Loyalty
- Wellbeing
- Happiness

EX needs a bit of a PR makeover—which we're trying to achieve through this book—as it's still often mistakenly seen as the 'soft stuff'. As you can see from the list above, it's not all about that. Like us, I'm sure you've read many case studies of organisations that performed well during the Covid-19 pandemic—on the surface at least, these were all people-centric organisations.

Getting back to the 'harder stuff' (and we don't mean whisky), we share the views of Jim Clifton[9], Chairman and CEO of Gallup, when he says, '... global productivity can be fixed. Executives and a wide variety of team leaders at many different levels could change the world's productivity quickly.'

What senior leaders need to understand is that the eleven things in the bullet point list above are an outcome of the everyday experiences of employees—be it positive or negative. And with payroll costs being anywhere from 15% to 50% of gross revenue, shouldn't you seek to maximise this cost? Do racehorse owners pay millions for a stable of thoroughbred horses, then give them little training, poor feed, and shabby equipment prior to racing?

BARRIERS TO OFFERING A GREAT EX

According to a Deloitte[10] study, 85% of employees from the US and 84% from the UK rated EX as important or very important. However, in the same study, they found that only 22% reported that their companies were excellent at building a differentiated employee experience. So, why is such a simple concept proving so hard to bring to life for organisations? Here are some reasons:

1. EX is not a priority for organisations, despite findings such as in the Deloitte study or Forbes[11] calling EX the 'number one priority for HR', back in 2017. It rarely appears on risk registers, despite the potentially massive performance impact of high employee turnover, low motivation levels and the like.

2. Most organisations have yet to assign a senior leader to be responsible for EX or purposefully assign employees to EX roles. Instead, they continue to rely on HR employees to perform EX tasks as 'add-ons' to their day-to-day role.

3. There is little funding available to improve EX. (We don't believe it needs a lot... probably half a Director's salary per year would enable a significant shift across an entire organisation.)

4. Employee feedback mechanisms are largely used to prove what's going right at an organisation, with topics and questions posed being biased towards the positive, with little appetite for digging beneath the surface to unearth real issues and areas for improvement.

5. Few organisations view the many EX touchpoints holistically. Instead, they're managed and reported on in silos.

6. Employees are often still viewed as 'the problem' instead of being seen as central to the solution.

If you're still not sold on why EX should, indeed, be a priority for your organisation, here's a few more stats for you:

- According to an analysis of 250 organisations[12], those that invest in EX are four times more profitable.
- According to a study by Willis Towers Watson[13], organisations with a strong EX saw a 4% growth in revenue while those with a poor EX had a 1% decline.
- According to a 2019 TI People[14] survey, effective EX gives back 100 hours per employee and manager per year on average.

THE EXO SURVEY

We wanted to dig deeper into what the issues are—as we'd like to do something about them—and so worked with the IoIC on the EXO survey. Over 2,000 people were surveyed, and we received responses from eight regions worldwide, including the UK (75% of responses), the Middle East, Europe, and America. In terms of size, we saw responses from start-ups to organisations of 60,000+ employees.

As with many, we like to use the Net Promotor Score (NPS) methodology. For those unfamiliar, the NPS (or, in this case, the Employee NPS (ENPS)) ranges from -100 to +100 and the score is calculated by (% Promoters) - (% Detractors). Each individual scores from 0-10. 'Promoters' score 9 to 10 out of 10. 'Passives' score 7 or 8. 'Detractors' score 0 to 6.

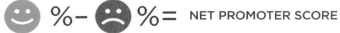

For example, the overall score answering the 'ENPS' question in the EXO survey:

How likely are you to recommend your organisation as a place of work to your friends, was: **-2.**

This is a reasonable score, as anything 0 upwards is considered fairly good. However, if those surveyed were all from the same organisation, there would certainly be room for improvement!

EXO SURVEY RESULTS—SELECTED FINDINGS

The full results are made available in Section Seven, but we wanted to highlight what we think are the key findings. The results clearly display that employees believe that having an effective EX will improve productivity. (Good job, really, as otherwise we would've had to bin this book!) And, as the Gallup headline figure tells, organisations are losing lots of money due to unproductivity. But with less than half of respondents believing that their organisation is committed to providing a great EX, and people feeling they don't have the right tools to do their job, there's clearly a gap here—or, as we like to phrase it, an opportunity. Gallup[15] really are a great resource and a study of theirs found that, 'Only one in three employees strongly agree that they have the materials and equipment they need to do their work right or that they have the opportunity to do what they do best every day'.

To hammer home the point, just 46% who responded to our survey felt motivated after going through the onboarding/joining experience. Imagine if over half of your customers felt deflated immediately after signing up? You'd want to do something about it. And so you should do the same with your people's start to working life with you.

SELECTED DEMOGRAPHICS

North America
7.14%

UK
68.45%

Rest of Europe
7.44%

Asia
1.69%

South America
1.19%

Africa
1.49%

Middle East
10.71%

Oceania
1.89%

ORGANISATION REGION

HOW MANY PEOPLE WORK IN YOUR ORGANISATION?

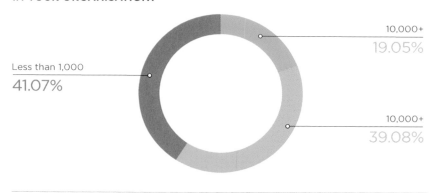

10,000+
19.05%

Less than 1,000
41.07%

10,000+
39.08%

SIZE OF ORGANISATION

WHAT KIND OF ORGANISATION DO YOU WORK FOR?

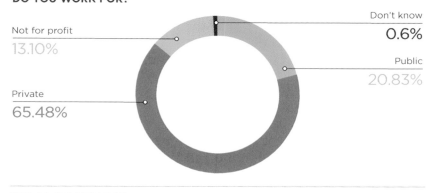

Don't know
0.6%

Not for profit
13.10%

Public
20.83%

Private
65.48%

KIND OF ORGANISATION

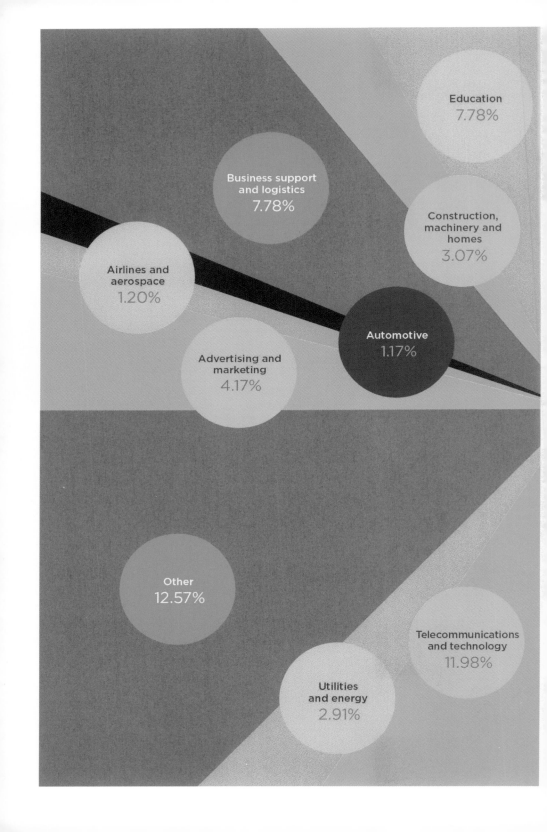

Education
7.78%

Business support
and logistics
7.78%

Construction,
machinery and
homes
3.07%

Airlines and
aerospace
1.20%

Automotive
1.17%

Advertising and
marketing
4.17%

Other
12.57%

Telecommunications
and technology
11.98%

Utilities
and energy
2.91%

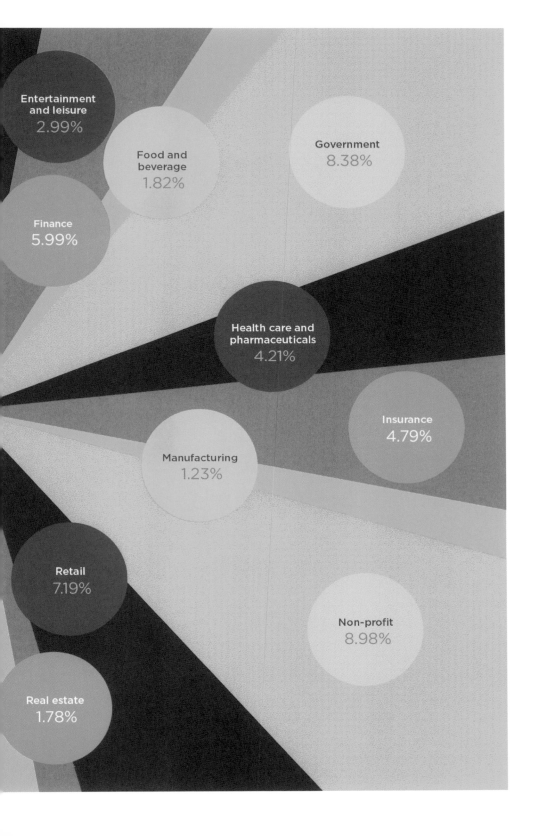

PEOPLE'S ATTITUDES TO WORK

I FEEL PROUD TO WORK FOR MY ORGANISATION

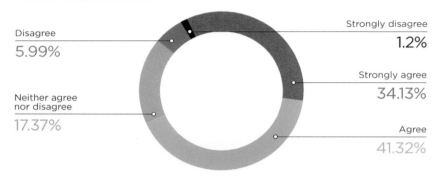

Disagree
5.99%

Strongly disagree
1.2%

Neither agree nor disagree
17.37%

Strongly agree
34.13%

Agree
41.32%

PRIDE

HOW LONG DO YOU SEE YOURSELF STAYING AT YOUR CURRENT ORGANISATION?

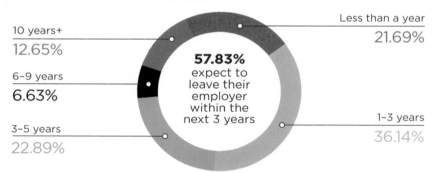

10 years+
12.65%

6–9 years
6.63%

3–5 years
22.89%

57.83% expect to leave their employer within the next 3 years

Less than a year
21.69%

1–3 years
36.14%

TALENT RETENTION

I AM MOTIVATED TO GIVE MY
BEST IN MY CURRENT ROLE

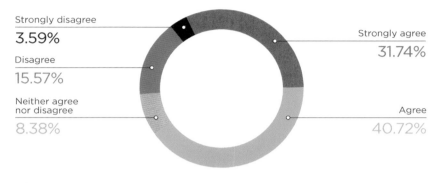

Strongly disagree
3.59%

Disagree
15.57%

Neither agree
nor disagree
8.38%

Strongly agree
31.74%

Agree
40.72%

SELF-MOTIVATION

The strong scores for pride (75%) and self-motivation (73%) show that most people want to come to work to make a difference. So, the willingness to work is there; the challenge is to get the best out of people. It could be considered concerning that 58% of employees only see themselves staying at their current organisation for less than three years. Imagine if this were one organisation? That would seriously impact recruitment costs and lost productivity—which is why internal findings such as these should be on the risk register. Our findings on employee loyalty are similar to the Gallup survey we mentioned earlier which found that 63% of employees believe it is 'very likely' or 'somewhat likely' that they could find a job as good as the one they have.

LEADERSHIP

I FEEL THAT EMPLOYEE FEEDBACK IS TAKEN SERIOUSLY BY MY LEADERSHIP TEAM

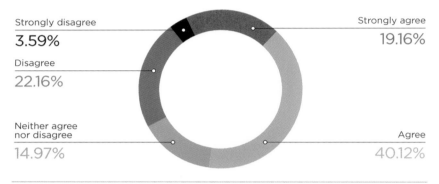

Strongly disagree
3.59%

Strongly agree
19.16%

Disagree
22.16%

Neither agree nor disagree
14.97%

Agree
40.12%

FEEDBACK

I HAVE CONFIDENCE IN THE SENIOR LEADERS AT MY ORGANISATION

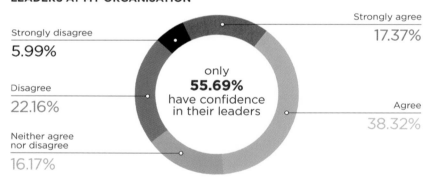

Strongly disagree
5.99%

Strongly agree
17.37%

Disagree
22.16%

only
55.69%
have confidence
in their leaders

Agree
38.32%

Neither agree nor disagree
16.17%

CONFIDENCE IN LEADERS

**MY LEADERS GENUINELY CARE ABOUT
HOW OUR EMPLOYEES ARE TREATED**

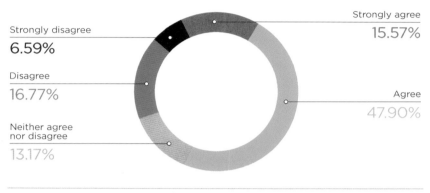

Strongly agree
15.57%

Strongly disagree
6.59%

Disagree
16.77%

Agree
47.90%

Neither agree
nor disagree
13.17%

CARE FOR EMPLOYEES

Scores for leaders were a mixed bag. Around three-quarters of respondents agreed that their leaders care how their employees were treated, with slightly less (59%) thinking feedback is taken seriously. What is concerning is that only slightly over half have confidence in their senior leaders. Oftentimes poor leadership scores are due to a lack of visibility. Is the story of the organisation being shared enough with the employees? Are leaders acting upon feedback or, if not, explaining the reasons why?

LINE MANAGERS

MY ORGANISATION HAS A CULTURE OF SAYING 'THANK YOU' TO OUR EMPLOYEES

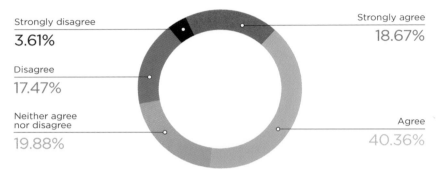

Strongly disagree
3.61%

Strongly agree
18.67%

Disagree
17.47%

Neither agree nor disagree
19.88%

Agree
40.36%

SAYING THANK YOU

MY LINE MANAGER UNDERSTANDS WHAT MOTIVATES ME TO COME TO WORK EACH DAY

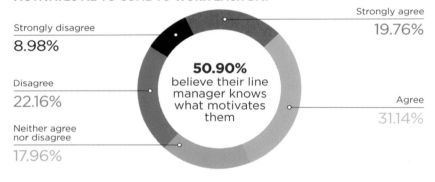

Strongly disagree
8.98%

Strongly agree
19.76%

50.90%
believe their line manager knows what motivates them

Disagree
22.16%

Agree
31.14%

Neither agree nor disagree
17.96%

LINE MANAGER UNDERSTANDING MOTIVATION

These people truly do have it tough. They have to please their bosses *and* those reporting into them. A cliché term for them these days is 'the frozen middle', but this group are those which require the most support, in terms of EX, as they own most of the employee touchpoints. With only 51% believing that their manager understands what motivates them, there is work to do. (Fortunately, we can recommend to tool to help with this, which we discuss in Section Three.) It's also clear that there should be a bigger focus on recognising good work. 66% of respondents to a Speakap[16] survey ranked appreciation for work as a high factor in job satisfaction and 94% said that their relationship with their line manager is very important or important. As the popular post on LinkedIn goes: people leave bad bosses, not their jobs. Therefore, the importance of offering line managers support in creating a great EX is clear.

ALIGNING EX AND CX

I AM KEPT UP-TO-DATE WITH WHAT OUR CUSTOMERS THINK ABOUT MY ORGANISATION

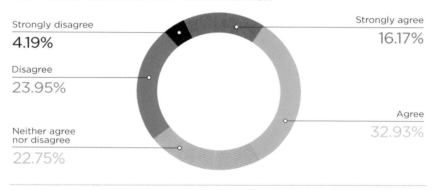

Strongly disagree
4.19%

Disagree
23.95%

Neither agree
nor disagree
22.75%

Strongly agree
16.17%

Agree
32.93%

UP-TO-DATE WITH CX

I BELIEVE THAT MY ORGANISATION IS COMMITTED TO PROVIDING THE BEST POSSIBLE EXPERIENCE FOR EMPLOYEES

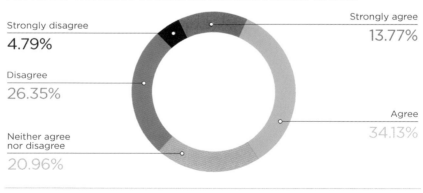

Strongly disagree
4.79%

Disagree
26.35%

Neither agree
nor disagree
20.96%

Strongly agree
13.77%

Agree
34.13%

EX COMMITMENT

45

MY ORGANISATION VALUES CUSTOMERS MORE THAN ITS EMPLOYEES

Strongly disagree
2.40%

Disagree
16.17%

Neither agree
nor disagree
28.14%

Strongly agree
20.36%

Agree
32.93%

53.29%
believe their
organisation values
customers over
employees

VALUING CX MORE

It's a great big red flag that over half of respondents don't agree that their organisation is committed to providing the best possible experience for employees. And as we think it's important to create a great BX, it's disappointing to learn that slightly less than half of respondents felt kept up-to-date with customer feedback. (Remember that EX x CX = BX^2.) If the customer is king, surely you would want everyone to know how they're feeling? Home[17] found in their survey that 49% of respondents scored EX and CX as either 'not linked at all' or that they have 'a weak link'. So, it's clear that EX and CX are not thought of as two sides of the same coin, which they truly are.

MANAGING CHANGE

MY ORGANISATION MANAGES CHANGE WELL

Strongly disagree
10.78%

Disagree
33.53%

Strongly agree
8.38%

Agree
20.36%

Neither agree
nor disagree
26.95%

only
28.74%
believe their
organisation
manages
change well

MANAGING CHANGE

MY ORGANISATION EQUIPS EMPLOYEES THROUGH TECHNOLOGY AND TRAINING TO HANDLE ORGANISATIONAL CHANGE WELL

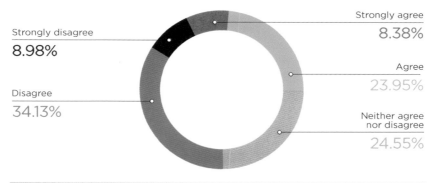

Strongly agree
8.38%

Strongly disagree
8.98%

Agree
23.95%

Disagree
34.13%

Neither agree
nor disagree
24.55%

TOOLS

I FEEL I HAVE THE OPPORTUNITY TO HAVE MY SAY ABOUT ORGANISATIONAL CHANGE

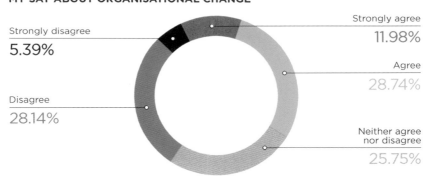

Strongly agree
11.98%

Strongly disagree
5.39%

Agree
28.74%

Disagree
28.14%

Neither agree
nor disagree
25.75%

HAVING SAY

As the cliché goes, change is the only constant, so it's very important to manage this well. According to our research, this isn't happening. Only 28% feel change is managed well and there's a similar score for employees being equipped with the right tools and training to make the change. As we come onto in Section Five, we believe we must co-design workflows with the people who actually do the work. As 41% felt they'd had a fair say in change projects, it's unlikely this is happening.

PRODUCTIVITY

HOW MUCH MORE PRODUCTIVE DO YOU BELIEVE YOU WOULD BE IF YOU HAD THE RIGHT TOOLS?

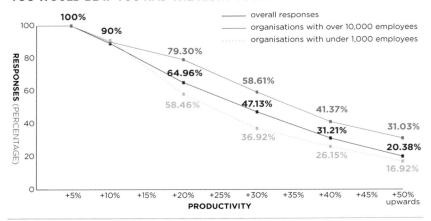

HOW MUCH MORE PRODUCTIVE

DO YOU BELIEVE THE EMPLOYEE EXPERIENCE HAS AN IMPACT UPON YOUR PRODUCTIVITY?

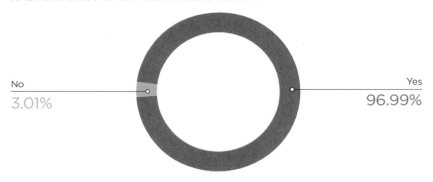

EX IMPACT ON PRODUCTIVITY

With 97% of respondents believing that the Employee Experience has an impact upon productivity, it should be a no-brainer that EX demands more focus. Especially when this underinvestment is called out by 47% saying that they would be at least 30% more productive if they had the right tools to do their job. And this number increases to 58% in organisations with over 10,000 employees where nearly a third of respondents believe they could be as much as 50% more productive.

THE IMPACT OF 2020'S COVID-19

HAS THE RECENT PANDEMIC MEANT YOU HAVE CHANGED THE WAY IN WHICH YOU WORK?

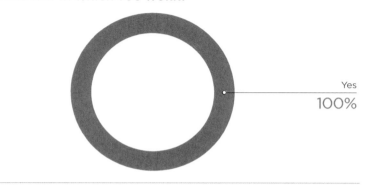

Yes
100%

CHANGE DUE TO COVID

MY ORGANISATION HAS BEEN SUCCESSFUL IN TRANSITIONING FROM CLASSROOM TO DIGITAL LEARNING AND DEVELOPMENT EXPERIENCES

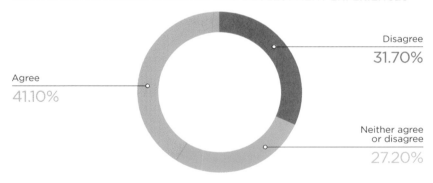

Disagree
31.70%

Agree
41.10%

Neither agree
or disagree
27.20%

DIGITAL LEARNING

HAVE YOU EXPERIENCED A DROP IN YOUR PERSONAL MOTIVATION LEVELS?

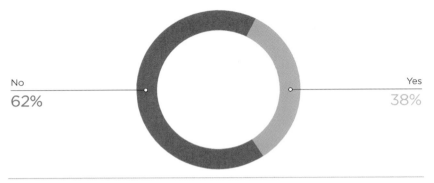

No
62%

Yes
38%

DROP IN MOTIVATION

WHEN OFFICES RE-OPEN, DO YOU WANT TO GO BACK TO WORKING HOW YOU WERE BEFORE THE PANDEMIC?

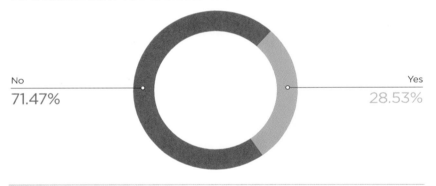

No
71.47%

Yes
28.53%

BACK TO THE OFFICE

We amended the survey halfway through to include some questions on what respondents felt had changed because of the pandemic. It's clear that a lot has! Whereas there has been great pride in frontline workers going about their business in challenging circumstances, there has been many issues transitioning from the office to digital. Most felt that their L&D experiences had suffered and about a third said they experienced a dip in their motivation levels. These things will need tackling long-term, as it's highly unlikely office-based organisations will return to every bum on an office seat five days a week.

What emerges from this is not just a superficial shift of working at one place versus another, but a conceptual shift from just 'turning up to work' to getting more from less. It's a shift from looking like one is being productive—at one's desk, responding to emails, attending meetings—versus actually being productive with one's time. This is the (very frequently cited but infrequently practiced) 80/20 principle of getting more from less. If this shift sticks, it could be a positive move away from 'presenteeism' and towards something more dynamic that also gives employees more freedom, autonomy, and 'work/life balance' Interestingly, the Gartner CFO Survey[18] reveals that 74% intend to shift some employees to remote working permanently, so some organisations are already reacting to this issue.

A PEOPLE-FIRST CULTURE

These are wise words from Richard Branson, which we make no apologies for repeating:

> *"Clients do not come first. Employees come first. If you take care of your employees, they will take care of the clients."*

For those that believe that CX is more important than EX we ask how can you can offer a great CX without having a great EX? In our experience, most organisations are like cars. It's easy to have a shiny exterior, with appealing colours and nice gadgets; but it's much harder to get the stuff under the bonnet right. And without the engine, the car isn't gonna work. Employees are the engines of the organisation, and they need the right tools and fuel to work effectively. A car with a spluttery engine can still look good in the showroom, but taken on the road, its flaws will soon become apparent. You can have the prettiest apps and websites in the world, filled with gushing words of praise, but if your people are disgruntled and respond inadequately to customer queries, then the shine fades fast. Of course, these days, many disgruntled employees will post their displeasure on websites such as Glassdoor, and customers will Tweet their unhappiness with your service.

Some old maxims remain true, one of which is: treat others how you would like to be treated. Translate this to the world of work: if you treat your people with disdain, why on earth should they treat customers any differently? If you value the voice of the customer to give you that competitive edge, why ignore the voice of your employee, which can give you the same thing? If you value customer loyalty, why do you not value employee loyalty? Both impact upon the bottom line.

On the topic of good old-fashioned manners, the 2017 Government-backed Taylor Review[19] not only highlights the obvious importance of people earning a fair wage, but also the importance of people being treated with respect and decency at work.

It also highlights that:

Taylor Review Highlights	How EX can help to tackle these points
While having employment is itself vital to people's health and wellbeing, the quality of people's work is also a major factor in helping people to stay healthy and happy, something which benefits them and serves the wider public interest.	The majority of employees want to be stretched and challenged, and to have meaningful work; by doing so, they will enhance their wellbeing. It's not only important for people to be happy in their job, it's equally as important to send them home happy. They do have a life outside of work.
Better designed work that gets the best out of people can make an important contribution to tackling our complex challenge of low productivity.	We're glad that Taylor highlighted the challenge of low productivity, and we believe that co-designing workflows with frontline employees will help to tackle lost productivity. Also, as our research shows, if you give people the right tools to do the job they will be more productive.
We should, as a matter of principle, want the experience of work to match the aspirations we have for modern citizenship—that people feel they are respected, trusted and enabled and expected to take responsibility.	Employees should be treated with more respect, their views heard, and they should be empowered to make more decisions.
The pace of change in the modern economy, and particularly in technology and the development of new business models, means we need a concerted approach to work which is both up to date and responsive and based on enduring principles of fairness.	Managing change is a hot topic for leaders and, as our research shows, employees don't feel it is currently being done well. Coupling the right tools with a desire for employee involvement and participation should certainly be an emphasis of EX.

CULTURE

Many people confuse EX with culture, but they are definitely not two different terms for the same thing. We see EX as the umbrella term, with culture and productivity being the two key pillars. Other EX commentators say that EX is about 'culture, environment and tools'. Needless to say that culture is central to EX excellence. It's important to note that your culture can accelerate or decelerate.

According to Wikipedia, the term of culture in the organisational context was first introduced by Dr. Elliott Jaques in his 1951 book *The Changing Culture of a Factory*[20]. The author is quoted as saying: 'The culture of the factory is its customary and traditional way of thinking and doing of things, which is shared to a greater or lesser degree by all its members, and which new members must learn, and at least partially accept, in order to be accepted into service in the firm.'

Sound familiar? In our experience, many leaders have still not moved away from 'customary and traditional' ways of thinking, and recruiters still talk about a 'cultural fit', rather than a cultural plus. Other accepted definitions of culture are often based around:

- The way we do things around here
- Shared assumptions, values, and beliefs
- (Or the more negative) It's what our leadership team tell us it is

At one end of the spectrum, leaders want to squeeze control of their organisation, and will refer to 'managing culture'. At the other end, leaders will be more 'hands off' and seek to encourage an environment of respect and trust.

So, why is culture perceived as being so important? We believe that it's because culture can energise or drain employees. Think of it like a professional football team before and after they sack a manager. Before, the players seem unmotivated, they don't press the opposition and passes often go astray. The whisper from the dressing room is that the atmosphere is toxic. After, when the new manager bounce takes effect, the same players whizz around and play with more of a smile on their faces. In interviews, players praise the team spirit and new ideas of the manager. In reality, it's the same players, but it shows you how a different way of doing things can work wonders.

It is our belief that you can't 'manage' your culture. Sure, the leadership team need to be largely aligned as to what the desired culture is, but it can't be 'managed' from the top down. So, senior leaders should enable a framework for culture through consulting with employees on aspects such as the vision and values, the Employee Value Proposition, the EX strategy and other aspects.

It should be evidenced-based and data-driven by utilising employee surveys, pulse surveys, focus groups, and feedback sessions. It's alarming how many ways of working are designed without asking employees—or worse—going to the trouble of obtaining information from Employee Voice mechanisms yet ignoring it. So, if you're thinking about redesigning your Employee Value Proposition, a great place to start would be asking your employees what's important to them. A great place to end would be to meet their needs!

PERKS ARE NOT CULTURE

Perks can reflect your culture, but they are not the culture in and of themselves. Too often, organisations play catch up, rather than innovate, and end up spending money on the 'in thing'. For example, start-ups started having hammocks and table football in their communal areas, then all manner of organisations copied them. But did these suit the culture?

These perks may (or may not) be representative of the kind of culture you desire, but they won't improve your culture in the long run. Provide free lunches and very soon people will accept them as a right. Provide hammocks or table football and people will soon become suspicious of the same few people that seem to be using them. And, there is a suspicion that organisations provide all these things to keep people at work for longer. It's much better to use your Employee Voice mechanisms to find out what's important to your people. So, if Wellbeing is important, then a Cycle2Work scheme or a healthcare cash back scheme would be money better spent than on an inflatable slide that takes you from one floor to the next.

We believe that organisations which believe in EX and its ways of working will find it naturally enhances the culture as it embraces employee involvement and participation, and helps people to see the meaning in their work. And, when people feel a part of something, they tend to be more motivated—and, hence, will be more energised to improve not only their job roles, but the general culture. And, as we've said before, happy hands are busy hands!

HOW HEALTHY IS YOUR CULTURE?

Some key indicators of poor health are:

- Employees wait for the senior person in the room to answer first in team meetings; this is then often followed by mumblings of agreement or statements supporting their beliefs
- There isn't much laughter or joking around happening, and social activities are poorly attended
- Employee survey quantitative answers don't match with the 'free text' comments. (We feel that the free text comments are usually the gold dust, as people have been moved to go the extra step to leave a comment.)
- People are slaves to the policies and procedures; these will come before the people side of things
- People are micromanaged

There are two schools of thought on how to assess the health of your culture. Many think, like Peter Drucker, that 'what doesn't get measured doesn't get done'; so cultural health should be monitored in key performance indicators, which make it easier to track improvements over time. Others think that you can simply tell by taking what philosopher Søren Kierkegaard calls 'a people bath' and walk amongst people. The truth is almost always in-between, so we'd suggest a blended approach.

To get the quantitative stats, you can regularly measure key points of the Employee Lifecycle through surveys and focus groups, and have annual and pulse surveys. You can have a 'people bath' by sitting in other departments, quietly observing how people interact, and noting positive and negative behaviours. Informal feedback from 'water cooler moments' can also be gleaned. Feedback should be regularly given to Employee Journey touchpoint owners, alongside suggestions for improvements. It's rather like mystery shopping for culture at your organisation. The way an organisation 'feels' is one of the most important indicators of engagement, bonding and commitment.

Statistics should be treated with caution, though. In our experience, the qualitative indicators are usually the most important ones as, let's face it, stats don't always tell the truth (as they're limited in their scope). We see this in ambiguous situations such as:

- Feedback scores from in-house training sessions could be great because the session was useful, or perhaps, because the trainer was nice and so attendees scored the session highly so as not to upset them.

- Where vacancies are swiftly filled, it could be that the role and organisation is appealing, but it could also be the case that the first person who came along was hired or that a competitor had gone bust and flooded the local market with people desperate for any job.
- In employee surveys, scores could be high as people are engaged, but it could be that those completing don't believe in the anonymity and so give favourable scores just in case it could be traced back to them.
- A low turnover rate could be because people are engaged, or it could mean an absence of other opportunities.

Our firm advice is to go for a blended approach to measuring your culture. Some quantitative, some qualitative; some stats, some feedback. Granted, it's swifter and easier to pump out surveys, but you simply won't get an accurate picture of your culture if that's all you do. Of course, it's important that you act upon the evidence. Organisations often pore over customer satisfaction surveys to give them that competitive edge, and so they should with employee surveys and other evidence.

IMPORTANCE OF BEING A VALUES-BASED ORGANISATION

If done right, being values-led can boost employee engagement, performance, and profit. If done wrong, it can lead to ruin. Yes, ruin.

THE SMARTEST GUYS IN THE ROOM

Let's start with a warning. If you have a spare couple of hours, there's a fascinating documentary called *Enron: The Smartest Guys in the Room*. Those in the UK may be less familiar with the story; in short, Enron was an American energy, commodities, and services company based in Texas, employing 29,000 people. Due to all-manner of accountancy fraud, the organisation went bankrupt in 2001, and two of its leaders were given jail sentences.

Enron's values were:
- Integrity
- Communication
- Respect
- Excellence

You will often hear it said that values should not just be something stuck to a wall—this is Exhibit A of not living the values.

IT'S NOT JUST ABOUT THE CHICKEN

On a more positive note, there are hundreds of organisations which actually do employ people who live their values. One such organisation which is often held up as good practice is Nando's. Their values are:

- Pride
- Passion
- Courage
- Integrity
- Family

(Note that, like Enron, they have 'Integrity'.)

The 'Nandocas' really do appear to work as one big family, and from our experience, you do receive service with a smile in their restaurants. Indeed, Nando's has been named as the best large company to work for in the UK.

With many of their employees unlikely to earn much more than £15-20,000 per year, it's doubtful it's the money that motivates their employees to perform. Nando's is famed for putting their people first, and have a saying: 'Nando's is not just about the chicken. It's never been just about the chicken. It's about the people who make the chicken.'

With 82% recommending the organisation on Glassdoor and an 89% approval rating of their CEO, they're clearly doing much right. A quick look at some of the reviews shows that many mention the great culture and that employees are looked after. They work hard at their EX and as well as an engagement survey, have listening forums which help to inform improvements.

Nando's is a clear example of 'it's about the people, stupid!' actually being taken to heart by senior leaders. It's definitely not the best chicken in the world, nor is it the cheapest; but the chirpy experience, created by the ambience and the employees, makes people come back again and again. And, as previously discussed, you can't offer a great CX unless you offer a great EX. And by offering both, Nando's has become one of the retail success stories of the last 20 years. (Yes, we wouldn't mind a free meal at Nando's—Mike has two teenage kids to feed!)

The vision, or purpose statement, defines why your organisation exists. (Some organisations have a separate vision and purpose statement, but surely this is confusing?)

Examples from famous brands include:

- **Starbucks**: To inspire and nurture the human spirit—one person, one cup and one neighborhood at a time. (We've kept the original US spelling.)
- **Facebook**: People use Facebook to stay connected with friends and family, to discover what's going on in the world, and to share and express what matters to them.
- **Google**: To provide access to the world's information in one click.

If the vision is *why*, then the values are *how*. The values should be shared, common beliefs that are treated as sacredly as marriage vows, or the fundamental tenets of a religion. It may sound extreme, but it's an appropriate comparison: consider how some religious institutions have come under heavy fire in recent years for failing to live up to their eschewed values.

Like Enron, you can purport to have all the high-meaning values you like, but they mean nothing if you don't act in accordance with them. Put simply, your brand isn't what you say it is, it's what you actually do. As brand guru Denise Lee Yohn[21] says, 'People don't want brands to appear authentic, they want brands to demonstrate that they actually are authentic in the way they operate and the customer experiences they deliver.'

When employees live out the values, and these are experienced by customers, you will attract and retain customers. When they don't you will at best upset them, at worst lose them.

IT COMES FROM THE TOP

Leaders must live the values not just day in, day out; but minute in, minute out. They set the gold standard for others to follow. What would it say, for example, if an organisation had a value about open communication, yet employees found out what was happening at their organisation via external channels first? Or if there were a value related to respect, yet the CFO shouted at her team?

Leaders must regularly communicate the values, and they should be embedded in everyday interactions. Announcements made to the organisation should embody at least one of the values, and people should be applauded, and possibly rewarded, for embodying the values, on a regular basis.

VALUES MUST BE FIT-FOR-PURPOSE

Whatever your values are, they must accurately portray your organisation. In a hierarchical organisation such as the armed forces, a value of empowerment simply wouldn't fit.

We recommend periodically reviewing your values; some suggestions of how to do this can be found below:

- Ask questions about your values in annual or pulse surveys—for example: *Do you think people live our values in this organisation?*
- Check sites such as Glassdoor and see if reviews match your values
- Regularly ask your employee forums
- Review how often values are used in communications by people other than the Internal Communications team
- Keep an eye on how many people are joining competitors who are likely to be paying similar salaries; if people are going down the road for a small increase, there's likely to be a problem

Ultimately, we think the acid test for your own commitment to your values is: would you fire a top performer if they didn't fit in with your values?

TIPS ON EMBEDDING YOUR VALUES

- Display your vision and values in prominent places in your offices —be proud of them
- Ensure they're name-checked in communications
- Recruit based on your values; ask questions which will indicate if candidates share them, and only employ those that do, even if it means waiting
- Reward people for good performance which ties in with your values; these rewards should be intrinsic.
- Ensure middle management are on-board with the values; Gallup's analysis[22] shows that the manager alone accounts for 70% of the variance in team engagement

If your values are fit for purpose and people genuinely do hold them dear, then this will boost not only the EX, as people will be facing the same way towards a common goal, but the CX too, as employees will 'do the right thing'. And EX x CX = BX^2.

THE FOUR ENABLERS OF EMPLOYEE ENGAGEMENT

We've already outlined the difference between EX and culture and, in some quarters, we have read that there is confusion in the difference between EX and engagement. Engagement is an outcome of EX. We do recognise, though, that for the last decade or so, engagement has sometimes been used as an umbrella term for the experience an employee has at an organisation.

In 2009, David MacLeod and Nita Clarke co-authored the publication, *Engaging for Success*. Three years later, they jointly found the Engage for Success (EfS) movement. EfS defines Employee Engagement as: 'a workplace approach resulting in the right conditions for all members of an organisation to give of their best each day, committed to their organisation's goals and values, motivated to contribute to organisational success, with an enhanced sense of their own well-being.'

Using an evidence-based approach, EfS discovered four common themes which are now called 'The Four Enablers' of Employee Engagement. Virtually every UK paper in the last few years, dealing with Employee Engagement, has referenced these. In recent times, some commentators have suggested that Wellbeing be added as a fifth enabler, but their importance as pillars of engagement has been rarely challenged.

Strategic Narrative

Visible, empowering leadership providing a strong strategic narrative about the organisation, where it's come from and where it's going.

Engaging Managers

Who focus their people and give them scope, treat their people as individuals and coach and stretch their people.

Employee Voice

Throughout the organisation, for reinforcing and challenging views, between functions and externally. Employees are seen not as the problem, rather as central to the solution, to be involved, listened to, and invited to contribute their experience, expertise and ideas.

Integrity

The values on the wall are reflected in day-to-day behaviours. There is no 'say –do' gap. Promises made and promises kept, or an explanation given as to why not.

If you want to know more about employee engagement, then we can wholeheartedly recommend looking at the EfS website: https://engageforsuccess.org/

THE IMPORTANCE OF A DEMONSTRABLE ROI OF EX

Peter Drucker's famous line on what doesn't get measured doesn't get done rings true for most senior leaders, and this is where EX currently lags behind areas such as sales or production. These two areas of work can easily demonstrate their ROI through increases in items sold or produced. So, how should EX demonstrate its ROI?

If it's not already, 'HR' should be featured on your profit and loss. By this, we mean regularly measuring and reporting on turnover and sickness. After all, both have significant cost implications. As we've already stated, we believe that productivity is at the heart of EX and we'll show how to create and track ways to boost this organisational imperative in Section Three. For now, we'll focus on two previously mentioned factors that you can report on right away to demonstrate the value of EX: turnover and sickness.

A turnover example

Organisation X has 1,000 employees and pays the average UK salary of £38,400. This means they splash out £38,400,000 per year on wages.

The average cost of a new hire in the UK is around 20% of someone's salary, so if Organisation X has a 20% turnover rate, then they'll be spending £1,536,000 on recruitment costs. (And that's ignoring losses in productivity.)

Just a 1% decrease in employee turnover would save £76,800 per year. A 2% decrease would save £153,600 per year. And so on...

If a sales person brought in a new account for £76,800, in most organisations, this would be wildly celebrated. We think a reduction in turnover costs should receive the same importance and recognition. Go on, HR folk, shout about such successes!

A sickness example

According to the CBI, the average sickness cost in lost productivity and cover is £750 per day. In the private sector, people take on average 7 sick days per year, in the public sector it's 17.

So, assuming Organisation X is a private organisation, they'll be losing a whopping £5,250,000 per year due to sickness. And, 'just for fun', if it were a public organisation, they'd be losing a mega-whopping £12,750,000.

If through an effective EX, which included a thorough focus on Wellbeing, Organisation X reduced their sickness rate from 7 to 6 days, then they would save a cool £750,000 per year. Again, something to shout about.

Turnover and sickness combined

If Organisation X could reduce their turnover by just 1% and their sickness by just 1 day per employee per year, they would save £826,800 per year. You regularly hear that support functions, such as HR, are paid a little less as they're not income generators... but this is proof that they can potentially oversee rather large savings, which are just as important as earnings.

This shouldn't be the end of the turnover story, though. It could be the case that you actually want to say goodbye to some employees as they're underperforming, or they don't match your values. It's true that there would be a 20% cost of their salary to recruit them and some lost productivity; but over time, in effect, it would be money well spent as a good performer who is a cultural plus would be more productive over the longer term.

Many organisations have a talent pool—and you really should obsess over the data surrounding these people. If you're leaking talent, then your organisation is unlikely to succeed. A very important metric should be the turnover and sickness of your talent pool, and it's imperative to keep these people happy and motivated.

We've been involved in pitching for numerous business cases over the years; these figures alone are a compelling argument for investing in EX; let alone the evidence outlined earlier that organisations who invest in EX are four times more profitable and enable productivity savings of 100 hours per employee.

However, as 1980s comedian Jimmy Cricket used to say, '...and there's more...'

TOP THREE TAKEAWAYS

 If the leaders of your organisation are not sold on the importance of EX, then do share the evidence that it positively increases growth and productivity. It must become a priority!

 Culture is an integral part of EX. It shouldn't be 'managed' from the top, though. Are your senior leaders enabling frameworks and mechanisms to boost and track your culture?

 Turnover and sickness must be on your P&L. By offering a great EX you should reduce both and there is the opportunity to make significant savings which HR should shout about.

PRODUCTIVITY —THE HEART OF A GREAT EX

IN THIS SECTION WE DISCUSS:

That productivity is an important ROI measurement of EX

The three Es of Productivity

The impact of motivation

Some theory behind motivation

The difference between personality and motivation

The Performance Triangle

The link between motivation and productivity

An introduction to a tool which can map and boost motivation

We ended the last section by outlining the cost-saving opportunities if you focus on reducing turnover and sickness. These savings pale almost into insignificance when you compare them to the issue of lost productivity caused by dis-engaged employees. To get the real attention of the budget holders, productivity needs to be the core component of the ROI calculation. Not only will the numbers be very compelling, but it will also help to generate a sense of urgency as once boards realise the extent to which they are missing out on the ROI from their people, they should be moved to act.

Through the ages, the question has been: *How can I make people be more productive?* The emphasis being on the 'make'. Up until very recently, productivity was gained through the threat of consequences. In biblical times, slaves in Egypt were made to work hard to build the pyramids, because if they didn't, they would be beaten. In the last century, travelling salesmen were ordered to sell a percentage of their stock, if they didn't, they would be fired.

Luckily for workers nowadays—by-and-large—the emphasis is more on how to encourage or enable people to be more productive. We believe the best way to do this is to focus upon the Three Es of Productivity.

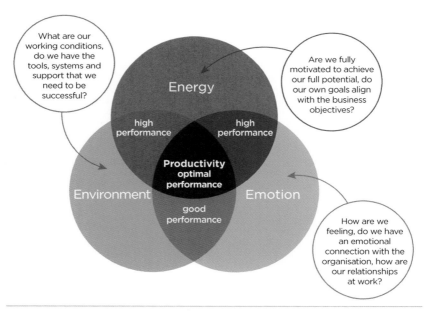

THE THREE ES OF PRODUCTIVITY

THE THREE ES OF PRODUCTIVITY

Energy: This is the motivation people bring to the role. The more energy people have, the better they'll perform.

Environment: This is the working conditions. What tools and systems are in place? What support mechanisms are there for employees?

Emotion: This is how people are feeling. What is their mindset? Do they have an emotional connection to the organisation? How are colleagues connecting with each other?

A metaphor

Think of the organisation as the vehicle.

> Productivity is the journey. Do people know where they want to get to? Have they been there before?
> Energy is the fuel. Is there enough to make the journey? If not, how do you obtain more?
> Environment is the route. Is it mapped out? Are lots of others travelling to the same place? What's the road surface like? What's the weather like?
> Emotion is the driver. Do people know how to operate the vehicle? Are they in the right frame of mind? Will they get frustrated by other drivers?

Of these three components, **Energy** is the easiest to swiftly improve and will generate the quickest payback. In addition, Energy is also one of the most essential components of any endeavour. Cars cannot move without petrol (gas, for our American friends!). So, no amount of clear weather (Environment), or well-planned route (strategy), or skillful and temperate driving (Emotion) will help if there is no fuel (Energy) in the tank! Energy should, therefore, be the starting point of any productivity improvements. Generating greater energy (or motivation) will also give employees more resilience to deal with issues around **Environment** and **Emotion**.

To be clear, to achieve optimal productivity, and therefore ROI, all three areas need to be addressed; but it must also be recognised that those responsible for EX can't do everything at once and momentum needs to be built through some quick wins that clearly demonstrate the value of improving the EX.

ENABLING A PRODUCTIVE ENVIRONMENT

It's always important to look at the evidence, and in Section Two we outlined that almost 50% of respondents to our survey believed that they would be at least 30% more productive if they had the right tools to do their job. Gallup[23] found that, 'Only one in three employees strongly agree that they have the materials and equipment they need to do their work right or that they have the opportunity to do what they do best every day'. This clearly outlines the importance of having the right tools and systems in place. In Section Five, we discuss the technical aspects of how you create a great EX which will help to tackle some of these challenges.

Sometimes, you do have to spend a little to get a lot. The trouble is that it's often difficult for senior leaders to understand the ROI on spending thousands on a new people-related tool or system. We come onto this is the next section, where we outline the opportunity cost of EX, which gives senior leaders some hard figures to work with.

EMPOWERING EMOTIONAL CONNECTIONS

The pandemic in 2020/21 brought about a greater focus on wellbeing in the workplace. Whereas once it was largely just discussed in passing terms—with organisations talking about the important of a work/life balance but doing little to encourage this—now it is becoming (thankfully) integral. Many organisations now have a regular cadence of wellbeing activity, such as online classes, content encouraging a healthy lifestyle, and support groups. As well as some concern for the individual employee, there is clearly a business benefit to them being fit and healthy as they're less likely to be off sick and more likely to be in the right frame of mind to be productive.

Workplaces are communities. And like any community, it's important to build a community spirit. As part of building a great culture, you do need to create opportunities for employees to connect with one other, both when on-the-job and socially. Although some people just aren't interested in having any kind of relationship with other people at work, most would at least like to have a few people to chat socially with, meet for coffee, etc.. These personal connections help to create a sense of belonging, which will boost someone's emotional attachment to an organisation. Isn't it nice when someone says: 'I stay for the people!' Opportunities to build these connections include:

- Encouraging special interest groups—parent groups, running clubs, book clubs and the like
- Holding corporate social events—pub quizzes, sporting events, seasonal parties

- Holding internal events to celebrate external events—product launch parties, religious festivals, major organisational successes
- Having mentor schemes or buddy systems
- Job shadowing
- Encourage people to stop the clocks for 15-30 minutes and meet people for coffee (in-person or virtually)
- Just go to the pub!

Like building brand loyalty from customers, you also want to build brand loyalty from your employees. A good starting point is to focus on the four enablers of engagement, as discussed in the last section. Employees will build an emotional connection with the organisation if:

- They know and understand the story and purpose of the organisation
- They feel they can have their say and will be listened to
- They believe that senior leaders say what they mean and mean what they say
- They have line managers who take a personal interest in them and seek to coach and stretch them

The role of line managers is of paramount importance to emotion. A bad boss can make someone's working life a misery which oftentimes leads to an employee leaving (which has a financial impact with recruitment costs) or being unproductive (which also has a financial impact). And, as we've seen via the Taylor Review, it's important for someone's general wellbeing to be treated with dignity and respect at work. On the more positive side, a good boss can make work joyful, which will positively impact upon productivity.

This does beg the question: if almost every organisation has a Learning and Development (L&D) team, responsible for improving performance, why on earth are there so many bad bosses around? We will say up front that we don't think it's all down to L&D; there are many factors, such as:

- People being hired who don't match the organisation's values
- People being promoted to managerial positions without being assessed for their coaching/leadership abilities (these promotions usually occur because they're technically good at their job or it's felt they deserve more money)
- Managers not having the opportunity to come together as a community to share best practice

- Managers only being given bog-standard off-the-shelf training (usually delivered in large sessions at a time suited to the L&D team)
- There not being any accountability for how managers perform as managers (if turnover in a team is high, are questions being asked about the manager?)
- The assessment of a manager's capability is down to the judgement of their boss (which can lead to bias, especially if they've hired their mate)

Later in this section, we discuss a tool which can give some insight into how a manager is enabling their team to be productive and, importantly, gives guidance on how to focus on productivity improvements.

MOTIVATION MATTERS

As outlined, we believe that Energy (or motivation) is a key pillar of productivity and, in turn, motivation is vital to obtaining a strong ROI from your people. If you work backwards, profit is impacted by performance, which is impacted by productivity, which is impacted by the often-overlooked motivation.

Motivation increases	Motivation decreases
• Energy and resilience	• Stress
• Happiness and wellbeing	• Anxiety
• Customer experience	• Frustration
• Relationships	• Absence and sickness
• Job satisfaction	• Talent turnover
• Talent retention	• Presenteeism
• Productivity	
• Fun!	

The importance of motivation and what it can help to achieve is clear. Achieve high levels of motivation and it will certainly support a high-performance culture.

FIND YOUR MOTIVATION ROLE MODEL

Think of a famous leader you admire. Then, think why you admire them. We'd be willing to bet that at least part of the admiration comes from the fact that whomever you chose is/was a great motivator.

An oft-quoted example of a great motivator is Winston Churchill. His speeches from World War Two are still regularly quoted today; and there is little doubt that his words helped galvanise not only Britain, but occupied Europe.

Someone more contemporary who is receiving much admiration for her words at the moment is Michelle Obama. Her book sold amazingly well, and thousands listen to her podcasts and interviews. Her words motivate and inspire people.

We both love football, and a great sports motivation story comes from way back in 1963. Tottenham Hotspur were the first British club to reach a European final. Their opponents, Athletico Madrid, were the hot favourites and so the story goes, Tottenham's manager, Bill Nicholson, was very nervous in the dressing room before the game. He kept saying how tough the game would be and what great players Athletico had. The captain, Danny Blanchflower, stood up and took the floor. He went right though the Tottenham team and said 'this player is great because...' and 'that player is great because...'. This immediately changed the mood in the dressing room and the players went onto the pitch all fired up and ended up winning 5-1. Several players recounted afterwards that it was Danny's motivational speech that was the catalyst for the victory.

It's curious that motivation is talked about a lot in sport and in warfare, but so little in business. Other terms such as engagement are talked about a lot. Imagine you were about to play doubles tennis, and your partner turned to you and said, 'I feel really engaged today.' What would that mean? Now imagine if your partner said, 'I feel really motivated today.' That would be likely to motivate you and lead to a positive mindset.

A classic example of how being motivated can lead to great performance is from the film *Robin Hood: Prince of Thieves*. The Sheriff of Nottingham's men discover Robin Hood and his pals regrouping in Sherwood Forest, and plan to attack. Many are scared, until the Morgan Freeman character, Azeem, stands up and gives a speech outlining that although outnumbered and facing an enemy with superior battle weapons, the Crusades taught him that it's better to fight with one free man than ten hired hands. Motivated by this speech, Robin Hood's men fight bravely and avoid a routing. Okay, this is a Hollywood film, but the meaning rings true.

HERE COMES THE ACADEMIC BIT

This is a book for practitioners rather than academics, so we don't want to delve too deeply into a review of motivation, especially when this has been rigorous undertaken recently, as in 2021, the Centre for Evidence-Based Management on behalf of the Chartered Institute of Personnel and Development (CIPD) published the *Review of the scientific literature on Work Motivation*[24].

They say that 'work motivation explains why a certain factor (e.g. financial incentives) stimulates employees to make an effort to perform their job'. The report outlines many motivational theories, some of which include:

> **Social Exchange Theory:** Where employees will repay kindness with kindness and are more likely to perform for a manager if they feel they are recognised and supported by them.
> **Social Identity Theory:** Where people are motivated to achieve results that are aligned with their social identity—e.g. people who care about environmental causes are likely to be motivated to work towards goals which seek to highlight/enhance such things.
> **Self-Determination Theory:** Where people seek autonomy, competence and relatedness.
> **Self-Regulation Theory:** Where people consciously self-monitor, self-evaluate and self-react; largely to act in accordance with organisational norms.

A whole host of other theories exist—two of which we'll discuss in more detail below.

We've already outlined the benefits of motivation; in order to obtain the best out of people, you need to understand what motivates them, as an individual. There simply is no one-size fits all approach. **Need theories** of motivation, such as Maslow's oft-quoted Hierarchy of Needs, display a hierarchy where by-and-large one level needs to be satisfied before moving onto the next.

Maslow's Hierarchy of Needs has been enduringly popular, and formed the groundwork for many motivational theories, including the basis of the tool we are going to introduce imminently. However, one problem with his theory is that it assumes everyone is working 'up' the pyramid towards transcendence. As we will come to see later from the research of James Sale—author of books such a *Mapping Motivation*[25]—in actuality, our motivations can fluctuate in either direction—and this isn't 'good' or 'bad'. All motivators are valid. But, we're skipping ahead! Let's look at another motivational theory.

Expectancy theory is more concerned with the cognitive aspects of motivation, and how they relate to each other. It is this aspect of motivation that links in more directly with productivity. It is lesser known, so we shall explain it.

MASLOW'S HIERARCHY OF NEEDS

Achieving
one's full potential,
including creative
activities

Self-actualisation

Prestige, feeling
of accomplishment

Esteem needs

Intimate relationships, friends

Belongingness and love needs

Security, safety

Safety needs

Food, water, warmth, rest

Physiological needs

SELF-FULFILLMENT NEEDS

PSYCHOLOGICAL NEEDS

BASIC NEEDS

VROOM'S EXPECTANCY THEORY

Vroom is often cited as the 'granddaddy' of expectancy (or instrumentality) theory. And, in layperson's terms, Vroom and other expectancy theorists believe that employees will be motivated if they believe that strong effort will lead to good performance, and that good performance will lead to desired rewards. These rewards can be intrinsic (pride, satisfaction) or extrinsic (money, awards).

According to Lawler & Suttle[26] motivation is a function of the combination of the following variables:

- The perceived likelihood that effort toward a behavioural or task goal will lead to the successful accomplishment of that goal
- The likelihood that the successful accomplishment of the behaviour goal will result in the securing of outcomes or rewards
- The valence of these outcomes

As you would expect, research shows that if people believe there is a strong chance they will be rewarded, then they're more likely to put more effort in. However, for this to work, the reward must be something of value to the individual.

People's motivation changes over time, and this reflects in work performance. For example:

- If someone were wanting to start a family, then money may become a main motivator. If they consider their salary as low and the organisation refuse to offer more money-making opportunities, their motivation is likely to slide. If this person were offered a satisfactory pay hike, then their motivation should rise.
- Or, if someone is a free spirit but starts to become micro-managed, then they're likely to desire more freedom. This could lead to them leaving the organisation or clashing with their manager.

So, what motivates a person today, may not motivate them twelve months or even three months later. It's important to regularly keep track, as motivation influences performance.

It's easy to calculate someone's motivation. According to Vroom:

Motivation = Expectancy x Instrumentality x Valence

Here's a worked example

Ebo's record for a half-marathon is 1h40m, set in 2019. In 2021, he'd like to run a half-marathon in 1h39m. Using Vroom's calculations, with a maximum of 1 for each, his motivation for achieving his record is:

Expectancy (E) = 0.9

(As long as he trains reasonably hard, and quits drinking for a couple of weeks prior to the race, he should make it)

Instrumentality (I) = 0.9

(He thinks the chances of receiving a reward if he achieves his goal as high)

Valence (V) = 0.7

(His reward will be self-satisfaction; this is quite, but not very, important to him)

Motivation = 0.57

(0.9 X 0.9 X 0.7)

So, his motivation levels are quite high, therefore, he's quite likely to perform and achieve this goal.

Now, if Ebo were offered £1,000,000 if he could run a half-marathon in a world record time of 58.17, his calculations would be:

E = 0

(Even if he trained full-time he simply couldn't achieve this)

I = 1

(The reward is promised, so the chances of receiving it are certain)

V = 1

(He'd love the money)

M = 0 (0 X 1 X 1)

Even though he'd love the money, the goal simply can't be reached, so Ebo would have no motivation at all to work towards this goal, so his performance would be, at best, half-hearted.

As you can see, motivation certainly plays a vital part in providing the energy to be productive.

THE DIFFERENCE BETWEEN YOUR PERSONALITY AND YOUR MOTIVATION

Unless you go through a life-changing event, it's unlikely that your personality will change once you've reached maturity. You can put on a front or psych yourself up to behave differently, but underneath it all, you're the same.

There are a number of different personality profiling tools out there, such as Myers Briggs and DISC Personality Types. These are sometimes used in recruitment to evaluate if the candidate has the right personality traits for the role. They can also be used once in-post to assess what kind of work and situations suit them best.

As your personality is unlikely to change decade to decade, it's not worth being re-tested with regularity. Your motivation, however, as we've outlined, is very likely to change with regularity.

THE PERFORMANCE TRIANGLE

Most organisations have strategic direction and seek to employ people with the right skills, but often they neglect the fuel in the car: motivation.

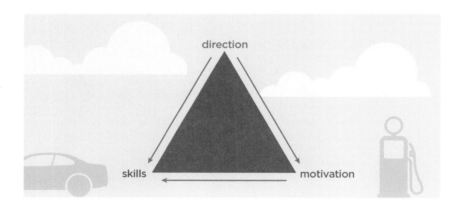

The triangle should be thought of like a three-legged stool: if any of them are not in place, it will topple over. As per the Taylor Review, people need purposeful work, with aims and objectives—both on an individual level and organisational. And, clearly, they need to have the ability to carry out a role and be continually coached how to improve. It's the third leg which is often missing from organisational and team priorities—the importance of which we're keen to make clear.

HOW TO MEASURE PRODUCTIVITY

If productivity is fundamental to achieving parity between EX and CX, then we need to be able to measure it as part of our ROI calculations. This can be challenging for many roles as unless there are clear targets and goals, like in a sales environment, productivity can be very subjective, and how do we put a number on items such as discretionary effort? This is where employee motivation can provide the answer.

As we outlined rather stirringly with the Robin Hood example, (and via Vroom's Expectancy Theory) motivation has a direct impact upon productivity.

Using evidence from a tool called Motivational Maps, which powers a platform we recommend called mojo—which we shall come onto—we have been able to see a clear relationship between motivation levels and productivity/output.

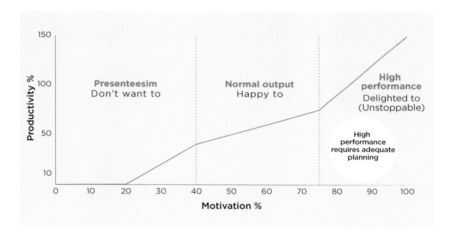

Normal Zone: There is pretty much a 1:1 relationship between motivation and productivity. So, if someone is 60% motivated, they'll be 60% productive.

High Performance Zone: Productivity can rise steeply and isn't capped at 100% as people can smash their targets. People in this zone can feel unstoppable.

Presenteeism Zone: These people don't want to be there, and productivity usually drops off a cliff. They can also start to impact upon the productivity of others as they can become disruptive, and start making major errors.

Highly-motivated people will have the right attitude and are more likely to embrace change. So, clearly motivation links to a high-performance culture. Being aware of people's motivation levels is important, as it will help to decide how to performance manage individuals, as outlined in this diagram:

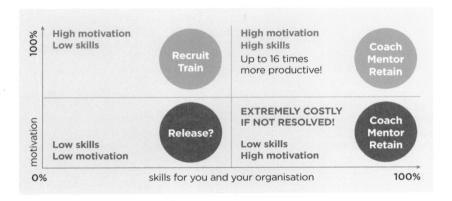

MOTIVATION VS SKILLS QUADRANT

The trick is how do you fairly monitor and measure motivation? Ask people to verbalise their own sense? Listen to the opinion of their line manager? Fortunately, there is a simple and effective way to measure motivation levels...

MAP YOUR TEAM'S MOTIVATION

Mojo is an employee motivation and productivity platform, which is powered by Motivational Maps, an ISO accredited self-perception inventory that not only provides you with a detailed description of what motivates each person, but also measures how the individual feels that each of their core motivational drivers are being met through their work. This provides valuable insights for the individual, as well as the manager and leader of a mapped team. The maps come in individual or team formats. Motivational Maps was created by the aforementioned James Sale through his extensive research into human motivation and the study of three primary sources:

- Abraham Maslow's Hierarchy of Needs
- Edgar Schein's Career Anchors
- The Enneagram, a personality profiling tool

Through his research, James has now published several books on workplace motivation and discovered that there are nine primary motivators that affect our careers:

Relationship Motivators

The Defender
Seeks security,
predictability,
stability

The Friend
Seeks belonging,
friendship, fulfilling
relationships

The Star
Seeks recognition,
social esteem

Achievement Motivators

The Director
Seeks power,
influence, control of
people / resources

The Builder
Seeks money,
satisfaction, above
average living

The Expert
Seeks knowledge,
mastery,
specialisation

Growth Motivators

The Creator
Seeks innovation,
identification with
new, expressing
creative potential

The Spirit
Seeks freedom,
independence,
making own
decisions

The Searcher
Seeks meaning,
making a difference,
providing worthwhile
things

It is used by thousands of people worldwide each year and both authors of this book became advocates for the tool after being mapped, and then became certified trainers. Brand Experiences has created the mojo platform, to bring the capabilities and insights of Motivational Maps to medium and large enterprises. Organisations have found it to be a proven and cost-effective solution to realising the benefits of increased motivation by:

- Providing a dialogue for motivation and continuous improvement
- Helping managers really listen to and understand their employees
- Offering personalisation, in terms of insights and action planning
- Focusing on strengths-based improvements
- And as we keep saying: increased motivation = increased productivity

We've quoted him before, and we shall do so again; we share the views of Jim Clifton[27], Chairman and CEO of Gallup, when he says, 'Make every workplace in the world strengths-based. The current practice of management—which attempts to turn weaknesses into strengths—doesn't work. Moving to strengths-based workplaces will change global productivity and growth overnight.'

To back up his own opinion, in a Gallup study of almost 50,000 business units in 45 countries, researchers discovered that workgroups that received strengths interventions saw sales increase by 10% to 19% and profits by 14% to 29%, compared with control groups.

HOW THE MAPPING WORKS

In short, participants take a 5-10-minute self-assessment, they then receive a score for each of the nine recognised motivators, as well as any changes in motivations since their last map:

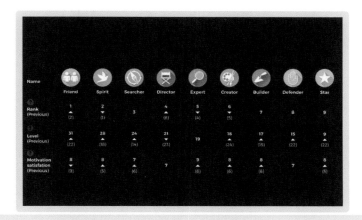

MOJO MOTIVATIONAL SCORECARD

There are a couple of key points to make about the nine motivators before we move on. Firstly, all motivators are valid and equal, and this is powerful in and of itself, as it gives employees a shared language to talk about their drivers without risk of judgement.

Secondly, we know what you're thinking: I bet most people have 'Builder' as their top motivator. However, in a sample of over 5,000 employees in 10 sectors, only 7.7% had this as their number one motivator, whereas 40.8% had Searcher as their number one. Truly, people aren't motivated by the money, there's more at play.

Dashboards can be at an individual (as above), or team level. In the example below, Searcher is the top motivator, which is the need to make a difference and find meaning in their work. Another way of saying this is: purpose is the most important thing to this person, team, or organisation. If this were the case, what does this tell us? Do the motivators line up with the 'values' the organisation has deemed important?

MOJO INDIVIDUAL DASHBOARD

Other metrics include the satisfaction of the Top 3 motivators, an overall motivation score as a percentage, and a Risk Index which analyses the motivators to calculate an individual or team's attitude to risk and change. The level, or importance, of each motivation is also calculated as shown below. There is more on mojo in Section Seven.

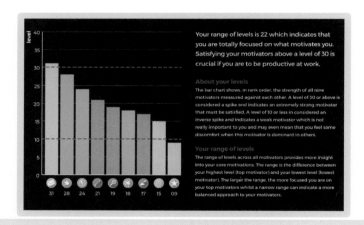

MOJO MOTIVATIONAL LEVELS

The old cliché goes that if you do a job that you love, then it will never feel like work. We're not sure about that, but if you have a job where your main motivators are met, then you'll certainly be happier and healthier. And more productive, of course.

TOP THREE TAKEAWAYS

 Does your organisation focus on each of the Three Es of Productivity? They're all important, but Energy is the one which can bring the quick wins.

 Imagine Serena Williams going onto the tennis court with low motivation—how would she perform? Now imagine her super-motivated to win her next Grand Slam. Do you consider your employees in this light?

 While extrinsic motivation—such as praise, or carrot or stick—can generate a short-term boost in motivation, the way to achieve long-term sustainable and renewable energy boosts is to tap into each employees' intrinsic motivations to understand why they come to work in the first place.

PROVING THE RETURN ON INVESTMENT (ROI) OF EX

IN THIS SECTION WE DISCUSS:

The importance of understanding the ROI of EX

The measures that catch the eye of senior leaders

The EXOpportunity Calculator™

How a small percentage shift in motivation
can have a huge financial impact

WHY WE NEED TO DEMONSTRATE THE ROI TO ACHIEVE PARITY

As we've said, organisations are simply more used to investing in CX than EX and will naturally assume that there's a stronger ROI for CX. Clearly demonstrating the ROI for EX is the only way to bust this myth and create a compelling case for EX to have parity with CX, at the very least.

We've already outlined in this book that an investment in EX can lead to four times greater profits, time saving efficiencies, and greater employee involvement and participation. But these messages are not consistently reaching senior leaders.

Departments, of course, compete for budget and CFOs will allocate funds either simply where they've been allocated before or where there is evidence of a strong ROI. We clearly see the value of investing in CX, but there's a wealth of uncertainty about the ROI and it's simply quicker and easier to shift the needle on the ROI for EX than CX.

Part of the problem in obtaining budget for EX has been a woeful lack of business awareness from so-called (or self-declared) thought leaders in the Internal Communications/ Employee Engagement/Employee Experience space. Courses on 'what to measure' focus on aspects such as views, clicks, and engagement rates. With this in mind, it's no wonder that other popular courses in these industries are around achieving a seat at the top table (which they don't seem to be achieving). Views, clicks, and engagement rates are of interest to comms people and can be used to assess the success of a piece of content. But they're meaningless measures to senior leaders unless the desired outcome from the communication occurs.

To give an example—if an organisation were to launch a medical cashback scheme, where employees could claim back for dentistry, new glasses, massages etc., then it would be of interest to the comms team to see how many employees read the launch story. But to no one else. This, if you like, is level one metrics. The next level up would be to see how many people had signed up to the scheme. Finally, the organisation would have financed this scheme and would hope that more money would be claimed back from it than spent on it. It's this figure that the CFO would be most interested in. This ROI would be level three.

Ultimately, businesses are mostly focused on competitive advantage, growth, and profitability—but these can't be measured via the fluffy stuff, such as clicks, views, and engagement rates. The golden goose is to correlate EX activities to the bottom line. So, measuring ROI = great; measuring behaviour change = very good; measuring views and clicks = is that the best you've got?

THE BIGGER THE BETTER—WHERE NUMBERS ARE CONCERNED

Individual campaign ROI success rates are one thing but to catch the eye of senior leaders in order to kick-start real investment in EX you'll need to do better than that. Using evidence from internal or industry surveys and data from other organisations can feel rather abstract to decision makers and so we've devised the EXOpportunity Calculator™ so that you can share with your own senior leaders the impact of a motivated, productive workforce.

THE EXOPPORTUNITY CALCULATOR

How it works

The beauty of it, is that it is not generic; you can use data about your own organisation. To get the most accurate result, you will need to have undertaken a mojo motivation mapping exercise at your organisation. However, in lieu of having these figures, you could do an indicative calculation using the average motivation percentage of 65% or even substituting the motivation % figure with satisfaction % levels. As there's no proven correlation between satisfaction and motivation, you couldn't use this as a 'real' figure. However, a substitute figure can help you to see immediately how the calculator works and the potential opportunity that comes from investing in your employees' motivation and experience. As we keep saying, motivation is integral to productivity, which is why it forms a part of this calculator.

Here is a breakdown of the different metrics the calculator considers:
- Number of employees: Add the number for your organisation based on total headcount
- Average Salary: Add the average number for your organisation
- Annual Revenue: Add the actual number for your organisation
- Average Revenue per employee: Annual Revenue/No of employees
- Churn Rate %: Add the exact number for your organisation
- Motivation %: The organisation-wide score from mojo maps
- Total Salary Costs: No of employees X Average Salary X 1.2 (to allow for employer NI)
- Lost Productivity at Cost: Total Salary Costs X (100%—Motivation %) = Cost of Unproductive Time
- Lost Opportunity / Capacity: Annual Revenue X (100%—Motivation %) = Unrealised Revenue
- Recruitment Costs: (Churn % X No of Employees) X Average Salary X Average Recruitment Cost
- Sickness & Absence Costs: Taken from the CBI calculations

In the first example scenario we have calculated the EXOpportunity for an organisation with 1,000 employees with an average salary more than £8,000 below the national average at £30,000 and average revenue per employee much less than half the average at just £50,000. While very low, these numbers might be more indicative of, say, a hospitality business.

EXOpportunity Calculator (ROI)

Number of employees ⊘	1,000
Average salary ⊘	£30,000
Annual revenue ⊘	£50,000,000
Average revenue per employee ⊘	£50,000
Churn rate % ⊘	10%
Motivation / productivity % ⊘	70%
Average sickness days per employee ⊘	6.4
Average cost per sick day ⊘	750
Average recruitment cost % ⊘	20%

Submit

Results	Value per annum	Value per month
Total salary costs Excludes pension contributions	£36,000,000	£3,000,000
Lost productivity (at cost) Cost of unproductive time	£10,800,000	£900,000
Lost opportunity / capacity Unrealised revenue opportunity	£15,000,000	£1,250,000
Recruitment costs Based on current churn rate	£600,000	£50,000
Sickness costs Based on latest CBI figures	£4,800,000	£400,000

Example EXOpportunity Calculation for an organisation with 1,000 employees:

As you can see, even with a workforce of just 1,000 people, generating £50M in revenue, and with them scoring a pretty good 70% on average on motivation, the lost productivity cost is over £10M per year based on an average salary of £30,000, which is well below the national average in the UK of £38,400.

The Lost Opportunity costs outlines the revenue that you are likely to be missing out on due to employees not being fully motivated. In this example, this is a whopping £15M per year or 30% of turnover. Big numbers, indeed, and one of the key reasons that senior executives should be motivated to take action.

Establishing a baseline

By carrying out an EXOpportunity calculation for your own organisation, you can establish a baseline and, importantly, identify the potential gains or opportunity cost. You should share this with your senior leaders and outline the financial impact of lost productivity and higher rates of turnover and sickness. The numbers really can be rather large, and rather eye-catching—which is the whole point. If, like in the dummy example, your organisation was missing out on millions, surely investing in EX would be worthwhile? Especially as you only need to invest a small fraction of the potential benefit to realise the opportunity. Depending on the strategy and approach you adopt, the ROI could be anywhere from 20:1 to as much as 100:1 which is why we believe that investing in your employees will generate the biggest return of any investment. And, as it involves your captive audience—your employees—it would stand more of a chance of success than gambling on prospective customers where an ROI of between 5:1 and 10:1 is considered extremely successful.

Quantifying the opportunity

To bring home the impact of changes in motivation levels, turnover, and sickness, over the next few pages, we outline some scenarios for organisations of different sizes. These should give you an idea of the scope of the EXOpportunity for your organisation. It will help you (and hopefully your senior leaders) see the impact that EX investment has, not just on improving the working lives of employees, but also on the bottom-line performance of the organisation. This is one of those rare opportunities where doing the right thing really does pay dividends.

EXOpportunity Calculator (ROI)

Number of employees ⊙	500
Average salary ⊙	£38,000
Annual revenue ⊙	£50,000,000
Average revenue per employee ⊙	£100,000
Churn rate % ⊙	8%
Motivation / productivity % ⊙	75%
Average sickness days per employee ⊙	6.4
Average cost per sick day ⊙	750
Average recruitment cost % ⊙	20%

Submit

Results

	Value per annum	Value per month
Total salary costs Excludes pension contributions	£22,800,000	£1,900,000
Lost productivity (at cost) Cost of unproductive time	£5,700,000	£475,000
Lost opportunity / capacity Unrealised revenue opportunity	£12,500,000	£1,041,667
Recruitment costs Based on current churn rate	£285,000	£23,750
Sickness costs Based on latest CBI figures	£2,400,000	£200,000

500 employee example

In this scenario, our 500 employee organisation is paying bang on the average UK salary and generating £50M in revenue giving it a below average revenue per employee of £100K.

Even with higher than average employee motivation at 75%, this organisation is still missing out on £12.5M of unrealised revenue. This means there is an opportunity to increase revenues by a further 25% without increasing headcount.

EXOpportunity Calculator (ROI)

Number of employees ⊘	2,500
Average salary ⊘	£40,000
Annual revenue ⊘	£300,000,000
Average revenue per employee ⊘	£120,000
Churn rate % ⊘	12%
Motivation / productivity % ⊘	65%
Average sickness days per employee ⊘	6.4
Average cost per sick day ⊘	750
Average recruitment cost % ⊘	20%

Submit

Results

	Value per annum	Value per month
Total salary costs Excludes pension contributions	£120,000,000	£10,000,000
Lost productivity (at cost) Cost of unproductive time	£42,000,000	£3,500,000
Lost opportunity / capacity Unrealised revenue opportunity	£105,000,000	£8,750,000
Recruitment costs Based on current churn rate	£2,400,000	£200,000
Sickness costs Based on latest CBI figures	£12,000,000	£1,000,000

2,500 employee example

In this scenario, our 2,500 employee organisation is paying just above the average salary at £40K and generating £300M in revenue to give it a below average revenue per employee at £120K.

With employee motivation at the average of 65%, the EXOpportunity for increasing revenue is a massive £105M or 35% of current turnover.

EXOpportunity Calculator (ROI)

Number of employees ⊙	5,000
Average salary ⊙	£45,000
Annual revenue ⊙	£625,000,000
Average revenue per employee ⊙	£125,000
Churn rate % ⊙	10%
Motivation / productivity % ⊙	70%
Average sickness days per employee ⊙	6.4
Average cost per sick day ⊙	750
Average recruitment cost % ⊙	20%

Submit

Results

	Value per annum	Value per month
Total salary costs Excludes pension contributions	£270,000,000	£22,500,000
Lost productivity (at cost) Cost of unproductive time	£81,000,000	£6,750,000
Lost opportunity / capacity Unrealised revenue opportunity	£187,500,000	£15,625,000
Recruitment costs Based on current churn rate	£4,500,000	£375,000
Sickness costs Based on latest CBI figures	£24,000,000	£2,000,000

5,000 employee example

In this scenario, our 5,000 employee organisation is paying above average salaries at £45K and generating £625M of revenue to give it a below average revenue per employee at £125K.

With employee motivation above average of 70%, the EXOpportunity for increasing revenue is a massive £187M or 30% of current turnover.

EXOpportunity Calculator (ROI)

Number of employees ⊘	10,000
Average salary ⊘	£38,000
Annual revenue ⊘	£1,100,000,000
Average revenue per employee ⊘	£110,000
Churn rate % ⊘	15%
Motivation / productivity % ⊘	60%
Average sickness days per employee ⊘	6.4
Average cost per sick day ⊘	750
Average recruitment cost % ⊘	20%

Submit

Results

	Value per annum	Value per month
Total salary costs Excludes pension contributions	£456,000,000	£38,000,000
Lost productivity (at cost) Cost of unproductive time	£182,400,000	£15,200,000
Lost opportunity / capacity Unrealised revenue opportunity	£440,000,000	£36,666,667
Recruitment costs Based on current churn rate	£11,400,000	£950,000
Sickness costs Based on latest CBI figures	£48,000,000	£1

10,000 employee example

In this final scenario, our organisation has 10,000 employees and is paying the national average salary at £38K and generating £1.1Billion in revenues, which still equates to a below average revenue per employee at £110K.

With employee motivation slightly lower than the average at 60%, the EXOpportunity for increasing revenue is a massive £440M or 40% of turnover. And this is before we consider the knock-on benefits of reducing employee churn, which is costing this business almost £1M per month.

MAKING THE CASE TO INVEST IN EX

As you can see from the scenarios, the EXOpportunity is substantial and taking advantage of it has never been more important or achievable. It is interesting to note that a seemingly small percentage shift in motivation and productivity can have rather large financial implications for businesses of all sizes. Armed with a compelling ROI calculation for their organisation, EX teams can have powerful conversations with senior leaders to secure support and budget for EX improvements.

Up until now, we've been focusing on the 'why'. We shall now move onto the 'how'. The good news is that you don't necessarily need to dream up an extensive comms campaign with clever slogans—you can just get started. EX is not one centrally-ran project; it's hundreds of little projects. If all you did within the first six months is to focus on the energy of employees, then you should see a significant shift in motivation and therefore productivity. To get started, all you need to do is a few sprints.

In Section Seven, we share links to an EXO Toolkit and other resources, which includes the calculator.

TOP THREE TAKEAWAYS

 Are you measuring what matters to your senior leaders? Clicks, views and engagement levels are only of interest to the vanity of comms people.

 Do you have a measure in place for the ROI of EX? If not, then try using our calculator. We believe it really shows the EXO.

 IT, Governance, and Finance departments use big numbers to obtain budget. And so should EX professionals. The ROI on EX is potentially huge and should attract the interest of senior leaders.

YOU HAVE GOT THE BUY-IN, NOW WHAT?

IN THIS SECTION, WE DISCUSS:

Key activities required to deliver tangible benefits to the organisation

A big bang approach versus an agile approach

Who you need in your EX team

Where to start on your EX improvement journey

The important things to measure

Congratulations! You have presented a compelling ROI to your board and convinced them of the benefit of greater investment in EX. The pressure is now on you to deliver results!

It would be nice to be in this position, eh? We are aware that boards have different approaches to business cases—some want the 'why' and the 'how' up front. You have had the 'why'... now it is time for the 'how'. Your first decision is what sort of project approach to adopt.

PROJECT APPROACH—BIG BANG VS AGILE

We are going to say upfront that we would recommend, where possible, adopting a more agile approach—where you do less, more frequently, regarding EX improvements— rather than the big bang approach of one huge project. There are many reasons for this:

- Big bang projects will typically have clearly defined starts, durations, end points and budgets. The problem is that when it comes to your employee's experiences, these elements would be impossible to predict without a huge upfront investment in time just to define the project—meanwhile no tangible benefit is being delivered. We believe it is better to spend this time delivering early wins and value. So, don't announce that you're going to build a completely new kind of aircraft from scratch—simply crack on with making enhancements to your current fleet.

- EX optimisation is an evolution not a revolution. In truth, it never ends. Rather than trying to deliver a specific project, it is really about looking to embed a culture of continuous improvement into the DNA of the organisation. This is better suited to an agile approach with regular iterations. As we've already said, it's really about 100s of small improvements. Think Dave Brailsford and how he improved British cycling with marginal gains.

- The bigger the project is, the more difficult it will look, and the more likely it is that it will be challenged by the corporate immune system, particularly if the organisation looks to be successful—even if it isn't realising its full potential. This happens as companies become bigger and they create bureaucracy that helps protect what they already have. The result is lots of rules and processes that were created with good intentions but have the effect of stifling any innovation or transformation. Think of it like a football team which has just won the league: rather than investing in new players and training methods to help them to improve further, they stick with the tried and trusted. Very swiftly, other good teams improve and surpass them.

- When you work in shorter cycles you can focus on delivering value to the organisation early and often. This helps to build a positive momentum for your EX improvements. 90-day cycles are our recommended approach as they allow enough time to do something substantial and deliver regular improvements to the business. It's also easier for people to get their heads around smaller projects. Later in this section we will outline what a typical first year might look like when broken down into 90-day cycles.

BUILDING THE TEAM

As you have taken the time to read this book (and have got this far) it's likely that you are either the person in your organisation responsible for EX or you would like to be that person. No one is an island, so you're going to need some friends to get the EX train moving and elevate EX to make it a priority.

Picking the right team to deliver EX improvements is key. You will need to consider both the core team that will be involved throughout the lifecycle of the project as well as subject matter experts that will be drafted into the team depending on what is being worked on. For example, if you were looking to improve the onboarding experience, you would need to involve people from your recruitment and L&D teams, and some people who have just been onboarded.

The core team will need to include some key roles that will help to ensure the successful delivery of any improvements and will be responsible for embedding a continuous improvement approach to EX into the DNA and culture of the organisation.

KEY ROLES INCLUDE:

The Evangelist

Likely to be the EX leader and responsible for promoting the success of EX improvements throughout the organisation

The Executive Sponsor

Must be a senior executive and have the authority to approve budgets

The Banker

Responsible for managing the budget and calculating the ROI achievements of EX

The Technologist

Will ensure that EX improvements can be supported with technology and integrated into the IT infrastructure

The Trainer

Will build the learning support for any EX deliverables

The Psychologist

Will look at the emotional impact of any changes

The Driver

Responsible for managing the deliverables against the 90-day cycles and keeping everyone on track

The Regulator

Needs to deal with any policy or compliance changes that might be needed to support changes in the EX

The Recruiter

Will need to identify and recruit the relevant employee representatives and subject matter experts as required

The Facilitator

Will take the lead in workshops and is focused on achieving the desired outcomes

The Outsider

Ideally someone from outside the organisation who can act as a sounding board and provide a different perspective

Right now you might be thinking 'that's a lot of people!' but, of course, it is possible for one person to perform multiple roles such as The Evangelist and The Driver, The Executive Sponsor and The Banker, The Driver and The Recruiter, or The Facilitator and The Outsider.

KEY ACTIVITIES OF THE TEAM

When you have the team in place, there are many key tasks that they will be involved in as you look to optimise the EX.

DEFINING THE EX STRATEGY

Although we are advocating a more agile approach to implementing EX improvements, it is still important to have a clear definition of what you are trying to achieve, so it will be a great first exercise for the team to define an EX strategy—or to review the strategy if one already exists or was developed to support the ROI.

Working on the EX strategy will also help to get the team on the same page by providing a forum to discuss the different views and priorities of the group and agree a united approach to move forward with.

As we have said many times, we see EX and CX as two sides of the same coin and therefore it will come as no surprise that the methodology we suggest for the EX strategy is the same one we use for CX strategy—we call it BASICS—and it goes like this:

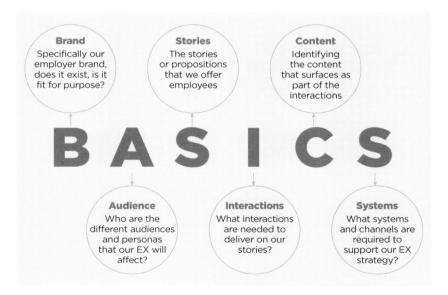

Brand
Specifically our employer brand, does it exist, is it fit for purpose?

Stories
The stories or propositions that we offer employees

Content
Identifying the content that surfaces as part of the interactions

B A S I C S

Audience
Who are the different audiences and personas that our EX will affect?

Interactions
What interactions are needed to deliver on our stories?

Systems
What systems and channels are required to support our EX strategy?

Depending on the scope of your EX strategy, you may be able to workshop these areas in a single session or you may need to break it down into smaller components; in which case we would recommend three workshops as follows:

> **Workshop 1**—Brand and Audiences
> **Workshop 2**—Stories and Interactions
> **Workshop 3**—Content and Systems

Your published EX strategy should include a high-level roadmap showing key objectives, milestones, and deliverables. During the implementation phase, activities that align with the strategy should take priority and the EX strategy can often be a useful tool to help resolve any conflicts that arise along the way.

As each EX strategy will be unique, it's futile giving you an example of one here. We certainly don't advocate a 'boilerplate' approach and think you should be wary of anyone who does!

STARTING THE WORK!
THE EMPLOYEE LIFECYCLE

Once you have your strategy, then defining the overall Employee Lifecycle is the place to start as this will define the potential scope of your EX activities over the long term.

Here is a reminder of our view of the Employee Lifecycle:

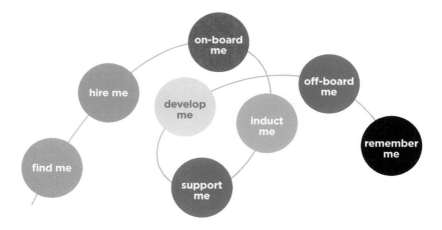

Publishing this internally will help define the terminology used for the different stages in the lifecycle as well as helping people realise that the EX starts before an employee's first day and goes on after they have left the organisation.

Core team members should define each stage, discuss them in-depth, and review evidence from employee surveys, Glassdoor, and other sources, to see what's going well, and, equally important, not so well. The Employee Lifecycle is also a great tool to help prioritise where to start either based on where the biggest issues lie or where you believe you can have the biggest impact.

MOMENTS THAT MATTER

It's important to identify the 'moments that matter' throughout the Employee Lifecycle. (Sometimes called 'moments of truth', or 'wow moments'.) These are opportunities to surprise and delight an employee and make them feel all warm and gooey towards their employer. They may be viewed as the 'soft stuff' but they really are critical points in the Employee Lifecycle that will have a huge effect on the EX and therefore employee satisfaction. In a fashion, it's not that different from personal relationships. A bunch of flowers here, a nice home cooked meal there, can really keep a relationship alive as it shows that you care for the person.

Compare these two examples.

Example 1: What usually happens

It's Abigail's first day. Upon arrival at the office, she walks up to the Receptionist, explains it's her first day, and says who she'll be reporting to. The Receptionist asks her to fill in a visitor's badge, says she'll call her line manager and asks her to sit down and wait. Around 5-10 minutes later, her new boss Katy arrives, then takes her upstairs.

Example 2: Wouldn't it be nice

It's Abigail's first day. Upon arrival at the office, she walks up to the Receptionist. Upon seeing her, the Receptionist says, 'Welcome, Abigail— glad you're joining us!' She then hands Abigail her staff pass, and says she'll call her line manager, Katy, who is expecting her. The Receptionist makes some polite conversation, and within two minutes, Katy arrives, then takes Abigail upstairs.

Both of the above examples cost the same amount of money (£0). Okay, Example 2 involves a little more input from the Receptionist, but all good experiences involve buy-in and a bit of extra effort. But the difference in impact is palpable. Example 1 is a rather cold experience. Abigail may well be nervous and the 5-10 minute wait will feel like an age. In Example 2, the Receptionist knowing who Abigail is, and seemingly having prepared for her arrival, will surprise and delight the newcomer; and the polite chat may well make her feel at ease.

Then imagine if the vain of Example 2 continues. What if Abigail is shown to her desk and not only is her tech ready for her, but there's another moment of delight! Organisations who are beginning to focus on EX often love it when their new hires post pictures on LinkedIn of chocolate and a card on their desk upon arrival—it makes them look like a caring company. This approach is very good, but it could be bettered. What if Abigail mentioned in an interview that she was a big fan of Eastleigh Football Club (as Mike and Nicholas are), and on her desk was a brand-new Eastleigh FC mug? (Available via the online store: https://eastleighfc.store/collections/gifts/products/eastleigh-fc-mug.)

At the end of her first day, much will be a blur to Abigail, but when she goes home, we'd bet that she'll mention to her friends and family about everything being ready and especially the Eastleigh FC mug.

RESCUE MOMENTS

There's a difference between a moment that matters and a rescue moment—although they're often confused. Again, here are two examples which illustrate the difference.

Example 1

For safety reasons a ferry has to remain in port for an undetermined period. The passengers are let off, but the crew remains. By day three, they're tired of eating stew, so the Captain gives the cook some money to buy some more interesting food from a local shop. The crew eat a wonderful meal and thank the captain. To them, this mattered.

Example 2

For safety reasons a ferry has to remain in port for an undetermined period. The passengers are let off, but the crew remains. Following pre-designed protocols, the Captain immediately gives the cook some money to buy some more interesting food from a local shop, as all they have in stores is stew. The crew eat a wonderful meal on the first night, and for all five days they're moored.

The first example is a rescue moment, which has arisen out of poor planning. Although the captain will receive some short-term praise, the dining experience of the crew over the days they have been moored is poor. The second example may not have the memorable peak of the first, but the consistently good dining experience is, well, a much better overall experience and displays that the wellbeing of the crew is consistently paramount.

So, it's important to plan your moments that matter and try to make these as consistent as possible across the organisation. Not everything has to be a moment that matters... focus on defining where expectations and/or emotions are high and match or, hopefully, exceed them.

Lifecycle Stages	Moments that Matter						
Find Me	Employer Branding	Job Description / Persona Development	Job Advertising	Talent Attraction Portal	Company Insight Platforms	Talent Outreach	Recruit-ment Fairs
Hire Me	Research	Apply	Interview	Offer / Rejection	Accept Offer	Pre-boarding	
On-board Me	Paperwork	The First Day	Company Induction	Vision & Values	Cultural Expecta-tions	Probation Starts	
Induct Me	Meet the Team	Role Expectations	Team Integration	Systems Training	Motivation Mapping	First Review	Probation Ends
Support Me	Objectives Setting	Performance Conversations	Peer Support	Employee Voice	Informal Check-ins	Formal Reviews	
Develop Me	Skills Training	Personal Development	Progression Pathways	Reward & Recognition	Motivation Reviews		
Off-board Me	Decision to Leave	Good Leaver /Bad Leaver	Exit Interview	Handover	De-commis-sion Systems etc.	Farewell	Paperwork
Remember Me	Alumni Enrollment	Ongoing Communica-tions, (news, results, jobs etc.)	Birthday Card	Alumni Events / Networking	Referral / Return		

EMPLOYEE JOURNEY MAPPING

The Employee Lifecycle is made up of several stages and each of these stages can include a number of Employee Journeys. In order to minimise the complexity of journey mapping, we advise to try to be as granular as possible, for example, focusing on the first day Employee Journey as part of the overall onboarding experience. It is really about breaking stages down into manageable chunks. As mentioned earlier, the core EX team will review what evidence is available and decide where to start. Whichever area you choose, the next step will be to map that element of the Employee Lifecycle in more detail.

Before we can truly understand how to improve an Employee Journey, we need to understand the current situation, so it is important to map the current Employee Journey in detail first. Journey mapping allows us to create a visual representation of an employee's experience at that point in their Employee Lifecycle, and would normally be created during a workshop that would be facilitated by the EX team and involve a relevant group of employees who have experienced that particular journey. So, using the first day example, you would have members of the core EX team involved in the workshop, as well as people from Talent Attraction, Onboarding, L&D, and some people who have recently just had their first day. As we often say, it's the people who actually do the work who know it best.

Too often, employee journeys are 'pass the parcel'. A person or a team do their bit, then it's over to another. This can make the experience disjointed and often conflicting information is given. This is why it's important to have a core team, so they can follow 'the parcel' from one activity to the next and ensure continuity.

When considering Employee Journey Mapping, it's worth ensuring these things are discussed:
- Which part of the Employee Lifecycle needs the most urgent attention?
- What's the goal?
- How can we keep the employee in mind?
- Can you match employees' wants, needs and expectations?
- What can we do swiftly and what may take time?
- What can we do for no/low cost, and what requires budget?
- Are we being too ambitious in terms of size/scope? (Does it need breaking down even more?)
- What evidence do we have on this journey?
- Do we need more?

Employee Lifecycle Stage: Hire Me			Moment that matters: Research—check out company before deciding to apply			
Employee action / outcomes	**Is the role attractive and suitable?**	**Who is the company?**	**Do I know anyone there?**	**What is it like to work there?**	**Are they successful and growing?**	**Are they a good fit for me?**
Interactions (digital, physical, human)	Job advert – role, responsibilities, qualifications, compensation	Visit company website, google search, visit store / offices	Check LinkedIn for possible connections and reference points	Visit glassdoor for employee reviews. Search website, google and youtube for video testimonials.	Companies House, news stories, Annual Report / financial statements, share price.	Speak to connections. Shared vision and purpose. Personality and vibe.
Sentiment or satisfaction	😐	😎	🙂	😟	😐	🙁
Pain Points (to be resolved)	Advert is functional but not exciting, no personality detected. Salary not clear.	Company appears to be modern and dynamic but no clear purpose to engage with.	Despite finding two connections, less than half of employees seem to have profiles	Very mixed reviews on glassdoor and not able to find testimonials elsewhere	Very little financial info in public domain. Organisation seems to be quite secretive	Clearly articulate and publish the Purpose, Vision and Values of the organisation
Opportunities (to improve)	Develop personas for ideal candidates and write job description from their perspective	Create employer brand with clear purpose and values to attract suitable candidates	Encourage employees to create LinkedIn profiles. Share job postings via employees to increase reach	Increase number of positive reviews on glassdoor. Create talent attraction portal. Day in the life	Increase transparency, demonstrate financial security and growth potential for candidates	Recruit for Purpose, Vision & Values rather than skills. Develop employer brand for emotional connection

Sentiment / Satisfaction Icons

😍	🙂	😎	😐	😮	😟	🙁
Love it!	Happy	Cool / nice	Meh	Surprised	Worried /nervous	Unhappy

TIP: When discussing Employee Journeys, it's recommended to use 'I' and really put yourself into the employee's shoes. E.g. On my first day, I would like all my tech to be ready.

PERSONA MAPPING

Where you have different types of employees that are likely to have a different experience, then it is important to understand their different needs, wants and pains. Many organisations create 'Employee Personas' and map the journey for each persona separately. Instead of using these, however, we use 'Employee Archetypes', and we'll explain why.

Personas are fine in CX where you may not have a deep understanding of your customers, and any attempt at 'humanising' them is useful. You should already know a lot about your employees, and should strive to have a deeper understanding of their mindsets, their behaviours, their values, and their motivations. In our experience, personas typically don't support efforts around diversity and inclusion and empathy, as fixed characters are created with a name and a face – e.g. Brian the Gas Engineer who is a white male, aged 45.

If we take the example of an organisation that has both head office workers and remote field workers, then it is important to identify these as different archetypes, as they will have different employee experiences and different objectives and challenges. If the field-based workers included, for example, care workers and maintenance engineers, then we would again represent these with different archetypes. In this case we might end up with: The carer, The fixer, The seller etc..

The idea of creating an archetype is to humanise different types of employees to help us better understand the audience we are looking to affect. Things to consider include:

- What are their goals, needs, and expectations?
- What are their challenges and frustrations?
- What are their values?
- What are their behaviours?
- What is their mindset?
- What are their motivations?

After all, it's about the people, stupid! We can then use these archetypes to inform our other activities, such as journey mapping to achieve a level of detail that is not possible when we treat all employees as a single group. Archetypes allow us to personalise the employee experience to achieve the best possible results.

EMPATHY MAPPING

We can 'humanise' even further with the use of Empathy Maps. When we are looking to map a specific journey for a specific employee archetype, Empathy Maps are a useful way of being able to put ourselves in the shoes of that employee at that moment in time and understand what is going on, both physically and emotionally.

An Empathy Map is a simple and easy-to-digest visual that helps us to better understand what our target users are: thinking and feeling; saying and doing; seeing and hearing. It can also help to identify any fears and concerns as well as their wants and needs. Drawing again on the first day example:

- What is Abigail likely to be feeling on her first day? Nervous? Excited?
- Other than where her desk is, what else does she need to know?
- Where the toilets are? When she can go to lunch? Tea/coffee facilities?
- Are there any cultural expectations?
- Is there a dress code?
- Is it clear who her stakeholders are?
- Can she work from home?
- What about any parental or care responsibilities?

In short, if an employee is likely to be nervous, then reassure them; where they're likely to be excited, then build upon this. Having all this empathy mapped will help enable you to create a successful first day. Empathy Maps are a key tool to remove any bias from your journey maps and keep everyone in the team aligned to a shared understanding of the employee.

TIP: Ideally before you start a detailed journey mapping exercise, you should have already completed an employee archetype map and an empathy map.

METRICS THAT MATTER

Ah, back to good old Drucker and his 'what doesn't get measured, doesn't get done'. (Sometimes it's fine to repeat yourself.) In short, we suggest that you focus your measurement efforts in two ways:

1. Improvements in mojo maps scores
2. Improvements in satisfaction of moments that matter (or a cluster of them such as the example we gave of Abigail's first day)

As we've outlined, our ROI model is based on motivation, so it makes sense for this to be the most important measure. If you map employees before you begin any EX work, then you will have your baseline. As the EX improves, we would expect to see a rise in motivation levels. Which—all together now—will improve productivity.

Of course, you need to start your EX improvement efforts somewhere and you'll want to track how this is going. Fortunately, you can slice and dice your mapping scores, so for example you could, over time, track the motivation of new starters. If you have different job roles in your organisation, then you should compare these in distinct groups too. Nurses in the NHS would have a rather different onboarding journey than someone working on the NHS IT Helpdesk, so it would be useful to know how each group feels. The mojo Team Map allows us to create these distinct groupings.

As you will have carefully crafted a range of moments that matter, it makes sense to measure these too. We suggest surveying people who would have been a recipient of these moments, (e.g. if you have worked to improve your employees' first day, then ask those who have recently had their first day) using the following three questions:

- How satisfied were you with X, Y, Z? (out of 10, or a scale of 0-100%)
- Why did you give this score? (free text)
- What could have been done better? (free text)

This way, you obtain a firm metric which can be tracked over time, and you receive the gift of feedback to enable further enhancements. Again, it's sensible to bucket this by job roles, although you should have an overall score too.

Eventually, you will end up with a chart like on the next page, where you have your important Employee Journey points defined and measured on an ongoing basis.

THE EMPLOYEE LIFECYCLE
—THE FIRST 12 MONTHS

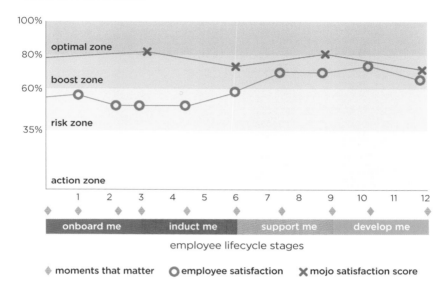

employee lifecycle stages

♦ moments that matter ○ employee satisfaction ✖ mojo satisfaction score

It may be that you are already measuring aspects of your EX, so it won't do any harm to continue with this, as you already have baseline data. But we strongly recommend focusing your measurement efforts on motivation scores and improvements to your defined moments that matter.

THE 12-MONTH ACTION PLAN

So far, we have talked about the different types of activities you will be undertaking to improve the EX, but we also need to consider what can be delivered over time.

We recognise that you can't do everything, and so have outlined below an example of what the first year might look like, broken down into 90-day delivery cycles.

90-day cycles

As mentioned, we are looking to deliver small incremental improvements on a regular basis rather than a 'big bang' approach. We would recommend breaking down the first 12 months into 4 x 90-day cycles with clear deliverables at the end of each cycle.

Every organisation will have its own set of circumstances and challenges which will drive the delivery cycles, but as an example, they could look something like this:

**First
90 days**

Setting the scene

- Identify & Recruit (internal) EX project team
- Develop EX Strategy—using BASICS methodology outlined earlier in this section
- Create campaign messages and materials
- Launch EX improvement project
- Recruit User Champions / Focus Group
- Undertake initial mojo maps
- Qualitative & Quantitative User Research
- Produce baseline for motivation of our organisation
- Calculate ROI for EX improvements

**Days
91-180**

**Identify
quick wins**

- Define employee archetypes
- Identify key employee journeys
- Prioritise archetypes and journeys
- Highlight 'moments that matter' (MtM)
- Establish journey mapping and improvement process
- Define success criteria and measurements
- Pilot process with first journey / MtM
- Update motivational scores

Days 181-270

Demonstrating early value

- Publish and promote results from pilot
- Expand project to multiple journeys / MtM
- Evaluate existing organisational culture
- Establish steps to 'High-Performance Culture'
- Embed design processes within relevant teams
- Publish regular success stories and ROI
- Update motivational scores (by taking another map)

Days 271-360

Implement continuous improvements

- Knowledge transfer to internal teams
- Establish multiple concurrent improvements
- Prepare budgets and business case for year 2
- Celebrate successes
- Reward 'High Performance' behaviours
- Update motivational scores

By zoning in on specific elements of the Employee Lifecycle, it will increase the chances of success. Trying to do something massive across the entire organisation will be rather more challenging, and will likely scare many people. By obtaining some quick wins, it will increase the confidence not only of senior leaders, but from the employees themselves. And by involving frontline employees in the improvements, it will increase their levels of employee involvement and participation, which should boost their motivation. Over time, if you multiply the amount of employees involved in these improvement groups, then that's a lot of engaged employees... and you'll be literally putting them at the heart of what you do by collaborating with them to create how the organisation works going forward.

In Section Seven, we give a worked example of all the tools discussed in this section, so that you can 'see' and understand how they work 'in action'.

TOP THREE
TAKEAWAYS

Don't go for a big bang EX approach. Instead, focus upon zoning in on important aspects of the Employee Journey (especially Moments that Matter) and make lots of small improvements.

Delivering an effective EX takes time, care and attention. Invest in the tools and knowledge required to map and deliver your EX and use motivation to create the right environment to implement improvements.

Define your success measures up front, and track and report on any improvements made... if it doesn't get measured, it doesn't get done.

LOOKING TO THE FUTURE

IN THIS SECTION WE DISCUSS:

Which department should lead EX

A new focus for CEOs

The benefits of integrating EX and CX into one function

How EX supports transformation and change

How EX helps to develop a high-performance culture

WHO SHOULD OWN EX?

At present, most EX activity is led by HR. As we've already outlined, much of it is as an add-on to someone's 'regular' duties. HR has been at the top of the people tree for generations. But given the appalling engagement statistics across the globe, it's fair to ask if HR professionals have the right skillset to lead EX. Look at your own HR people—are they more about people or policing? If the latter, they're unlikely to succeed with designing an effective EX. And given the disparity in funding and profile between EX and CX, HR has clearly failed to make the case for EX up until this point.

As EX is about putting people at the heart of an organisation, only 'people-people' should be given responsibility for it. These people could come from HR (as we know that many great HR people exist), Internal Communications, L&D or even Customer Service (especially as many of the EX principles come from CX).

We predict that, over time, the hierarchy of people functions will change, with EX as the umbrella and HR sitting alongside the likes of L&D and Internal Communications. The person with the seat at the top table will be an EX professional with a background in improving people productivity. After all, as we keep saying, it's about the people, stupid!

THE RISE OF THE CHIEF EXPERIENCE OFFICER (CEO)

What could be more important for a CEO to focus on than the brand and how the brand treats its key stakeholders such as customers, employees, and shareholders? We believe the CEO should be responsible for the brand—but before he/she is they need to understand the need for parity between EX and CX.

Let the finance team manage the numbers, let sales be responsible for revenue. If the CEO focuses on optimising the experiences that are delivered to all stakeholders, then this can only create incremental improvements in the performance.

Should, then, the title of Chief Executive Officer change to Chief Experience Officer? Is that not more reflective of what the role entails in a modern business environment?

Let's face it, many products are very similar, it's the experience that makes the difference. As the famous Maya Angelou quote goes:

"I've learned that people will forget what you said, people will forget what you did, but people will never forget how you made them feel."

WHY YOU SHOULD APPOINT AN EX LEAD

We recognise that it will take some time before CEOs come around to the idea of becoming the Chief Experience Officer. So, in the short term, we strongly suggest organisations appoint an EX lead. After all, other departments have them. Somebody needs to be accountable, and to report on EX activity to the boardroom—just like a CX lead does. Reasons why an EX lead is required includes:

- To improve organisational performance, and to report on this
- To drum up support and help employees see the benefits of EX
- To move EX from being purely tactical to being strategic
- To understand employee's needs and to deliver against them
- To prioritise EX activity
- To allocate resources accordingly
- To represent employees in the boardroom

INTEGRATING EX AND CX

As EX & CX are two sides of the same coin, we believe that, eventually, the teams looking after employees and customers should be integrated. They both create a competitive advantage and as many workflows are similar, both disciplines could work with and complement each other. Like EX, CX impacts upon the bottom line. According to Bain & Company[28], CX leading organisations grow revenues 4%—8% above their market average.

Brand guru Denise Lee Yohn[29] outlines the requirement for integration, but also that parity is required: 'Companies that emphasize EX over CX could end up with well-meaning employees who have no idea how to serve customers—or employees who are happy and satisfied but don't produce the right results. And companies that focus on CX without attending to EX could struggle with labour costs due to high employee turnover and a lack of creative thinking. Or a leader could wake up to find her company in the news because a disgruntled employee decided to post a video about the horrible working conditions they have to endure.'

We accept that it may appear somewhat strange to have spent much of this book arguing for EX to have more prominence and discussing how it will be completing with other areas, including CX, for budget, then to discuss combining both disciplines. But our point is that EX isn't on the radar of many senior leaders and so they wouldn't see the value of integrating the functions as EX is seen as being of little importance. EX and CX should come together as equals. We fully recognise that there could be political and practical considerations (or bun fights), but it is about creating the best brand experience possible.

Ultimately, we would expect EX (or combined EX & CX) teams to have more prominence within an organisation and EX and CX leads (or a combined lead) should report directly to the CEO. A lead for EX/CX could be called: The Brand Experience Officer (BEO).

ENABLING TRANSFORMATION & INNOVATION

As we know, the only constant is change and therefore transformation and innovation have become key components of most organisations' strategies. However, many of these initiatives are failing to deliver the desired results. Some organisations will buy other organisations to innovate, but not all will be in that fortunate position!

A topic which people hit on all the time is senior leadership buy-in. Clearly, any major changes need the support of all leaders as otherwise the work may not receive the priority it deserves. This alignment is always an early task for any major project. You really do need senior leaders to be facing the same direction, singing from the same hymn sheet, and any other cliché relating to alignment that you can think of!

A major issue we have found over the years is that, broadly speaking, you can split senior leaders into two types: those who seek improvement and those who seek comfort. The former are likely to embrace ideas for change and will willingly offer opinions. The latter are likely to block any moves to change workflows in their area of responsibility—as it will mean they have to spend time and effort getting to know and understand something new. Oftentimes even overwhelming evidence doesn't budge the 'we've always done it this way' brigade; and so it's vital to win over the CEO to any proposals to enable them to bring these people into line. (We would question why these kinds of people would form part of a modern leadership team, but that's a conversation for another forum.) To bring in another cliché, we disagree with the line 'if it ain't broke then why fix it' as *all* workflows can be improved, especially with so many ongoing changes in all marketplaces. As we've outlined, it's more about 100s of tiny changes than a few big bang ones, so a constant improvement mindset is important. Some business managers refer to this as a 'kaizen' approach of improvement; kaizen originated in Japan, inspired by the Taoist philosophy that 'a journey of a thousand miles begins with a single step'.

A study conducted by the Project Management Institute[30] (PMI) revealed that, 'Ineffective communications is the primary contributor to project failure one third of the time and had a negative impact on project success more than half the time.' As change is the only constant, and with a rise in homeworking, this figure will only rise unless tackled effectively.

Statistics such as these lead organisations to create not only comms strategies, but often big internal comms campaigns to highlight the importance of the change or transformational project. Broadly speaking, these awareness campaigns are a good idea and galvanise people behind a banner, if done well. However, well-intended words and powerful graphics will have little impact over time if employees feel that the change is being done *to* them. Too often project groups or external consultants sit in rooms and devise workflows without consulting those who know and understand the challenge best: those who undertake the work. Not being involved in change projects which impact their work is a demotivator for employees, and will lead to not only a lack of engagement in the project, but with a lack of engagement with their role in general and the organisation. It will also lead to a lack of adoption and advocacy for the change.

The approaches we outlined in Section Five and other areas of this book will be a significant factor in creating an environment where transformation and innovation can be embraced and deliver their intended results. By recruiting those who actually do the work into the Sprints, then not only will you get their buy-in and advocacy, but you'll also get a heap of new ideas to further improve the workflow. Motivated and engaged employees will want to pro-actively improve their own performance which, in turn, will boost organisational performance.

The great thing about EX when it's embedded is that employees are used to constantly seeking improvements, so will be more receptive to change—especially as they'll know that they'll be part of designing new workflows. This will then lead to them championing the changes, which will help with user adoption.

DEVELOPING A HIGH-PERFORMANCE CULTURE

It seems that every organisation is looking to create a high-performance culture and it is obvious that employees and their relationship with the organisation is fundamental to that goal.

Delivering the ROI potential outlined in this book will, in our opinion, be the best step that any organisation can take to achieving a high-performance culture. Remember that 'rubbish in' leads to 'rubbish out'. You need a highly-motivated and engaged workforce to achieve high-performance.

Engaging employees takes work, commitment, and buy-in, but it's not impossible to achieve. Exceptional workplaces share common philosophies and practices, such as values and ways of working, which can be tailored to all organisations.

As you would expect, there are a number of different models and approaches out there which aim to deliver a high-performance culture. The Hard-Girling Integrated Improvement Model[31] describes an integrated framework of three primary conceptual areas: Leadership, Engagement, and Wellbeing. It stresses the importance of 'inter-relationships that drive a high-performing culture and look to integrate all the functions.'

This thinking mirrors ours, as we have outlined that silos are the enemy of change and that at present EX activities are usually undertaken in distinct groups; the outcomes of which mirror the personality of the leader. Like EX, this model requires the sponsorship and commitment of senior leaders. (Doesn't everything?)

McKinsey & Company[32] talk about nine outcomes which will deliver a high-performance culture: direction, innovation and learning, leadership, co-ordination and control, capabilities, motivation, work environment, accountability and external orientation. We're especially pleased that they list motivation!

From our experience, some of the things organisations require to achieve a high-performance culture include:

- Commitment from senior leaders to prioritise employee performance
- Senior leaders to role model the values and good behaviours, and contribute to improving working practices
- Regular and transparent updates on organisational performance, including customer and employee metrics
- Support for line managers to effectively lead their teams and focus upon creating highly motivated and engaged teams
- Holding project leads and managers responsible for outcomes
- Being outcome—not output—based
- Having effective performance tracking tools, both for project and for individual employees
- Making clear what's expected of employees and why they're asked to perform tasks
- Having a fair and consistent approach to performance management
- Introducing a values-based approach to recruitment
- Promoting a recognition culture
- Establishing effective employee voice mechanisms

- Involving those who do the work to be involved in any discussions on improving work practices
- A commitment to learning and development for employees at all levels

Whichever your high-performance model of choice is, there's no doubt that an effective EX will lead to improvements in performance. After all, EX is:

"The entire relationship between employee and employer. It encompasses every interaction and touchpoint at every stage of the Employee Lifecycle."

TOP THREE
TAKEAWAYS

 Like every function, EX needs an owner. This person can then be accountable for all EX activity and enable inter-departmental working

 As the disciplines have many things in common, you may wish to consider integrating your EX and CX teams

 EX is fundamental to transformation, change and high-performance

SECTION 7

THE EXO TOOLKIT

IN THIS SECTION WE DISCUSS:

The EXOpportunity Calculator

The Brand Experiences Map

The Employee Archetype Template

The Empathy Map Template

The Employee Lifecycle and Journey Map Templates

The Stop, Start, Continue, Change Canvas

The Mojo Motivational Dashboard

AS THE PURPOSE OF THIS BOOK IS TO BOTH:

- Help you prove the ROI for EX investment
- Provide practical help to improve peoples' working lives

We are excited to share our EXO Toolkit with you. It contains a number of tools and templates that will help you to implement the ideas contained in the book, including the following:

THE EMPLOYEE EXPERIENCE OPPORTUNITY & ROI CALCULATOR

Senior leaders and budget holders love numbers and the EXO & ROI Calculator will allow you to build a business case based on your specific organisation that is backed up with real numbers. It is available as an online calculator and was used to provide the business case illustrations contained in this book.

EXOpportunity Calculator (ROI)

Number of employees ⊘	
Average salary ⊘	
Annual revenue ⊘	
Average revenue per employee ⊘	
Churn rate % ⊘	
Motivation / productivity % ⊘	
Average sickness days per employee ⊘	
Average cost per sick day ⊘	
Average recruitment cost % ⊘	

Submit

Results	Value per annum	Value per month
Total salary costs Excludes pension contributions	£	£
Lost productivity (at cost) Cost of unproductive time	£	£
Lost opportunity / capacity Unrealised revenue opportunity	£	£
Recruitment costs Based on current churn rate	£	£
Sickness costs Based on latest CBI figures	£	£

THE BRAND EXPERIENCES MAP

This shows the overall relationship between an organisation and its employees and customers. It is useful in helping to explain the relationship between EX and CX, and discussing strategic objectives and priorities.

EXPERIENCE DESIGN TOOLS

The EXO Toolkit includes templates to help define and improve your organisation's employee experiences.

EMPLOYEE ARCHETYPE TEMPLATE

A key part of improving the employee experience is understanding the different types of employees within your organisation.

The Employee Archetype Template allows you to build a representation of each different type of employee and build a better understanding of their hopes and aspirations, fears and concerns, needs and wants.

When looking to define or design employee journeys it is helpful to do this from the perspective of a single employee archetype to ensure that your employee experiences are as relevant as possible and personalised to the specific needs of each type of employee.

EMPLOYEE ARCHETYPE TEMPLATE

Description
Core purpose

Needs	Wants	Pains
....	....	....
....	....	....
....	....	....

Values—even over statements

1. ....
2. ....
3. ....
4. ....

Mindsets		Behaviours	
Strategic	Tactical	Introvert	Extrovert
Purpose	Reward	Passive	Active
Growth	Fixed	Reactive	Proactive
Optimistic	Pessimistic	DIY	Delegate
Team	Individual	Follows process	Bypasses process
High level	Detail	Satisifed with tools	Dissatisifed with tools
Short term	Long term	Focused on speed	Focused on quality

Motivations (H=High, L=Low)

Relationship		Wants		Pains	
Defender		Builder		Spirit	
Friend		Expert		Creator	
Star		Director		Searcher	

EMPATHY MAP TEMPLATE

Empathy Maps build on Employee Archetypes and force us to put ourselves in the shoes of a particular persona to consider their emotional responses during specific employee experiences.

Empathy Maps are about getting inside the head of your employees to understand what they might be saying, thinking, doing or feeling during an experience.

The Empathy Map Template can either be used by the EX team to discuss ideas or can be used as a prompt when interviewing employees about their experiences.

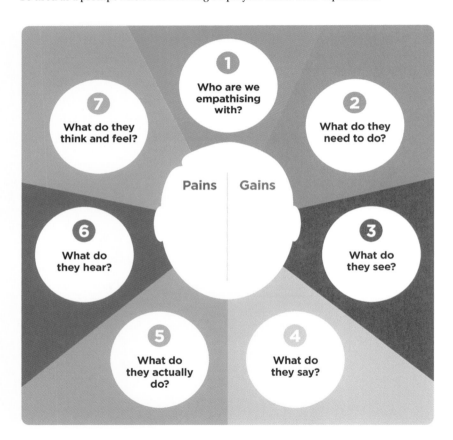

EMPLOYEE LIFECYCLE TEMPLATE

As mentioned previously in this book, the Employee Lifecycle encompasses every interaction between an employee and an organisation, which covers a huge number of processes, journeys and experiences.

Before we start drilling down into individual employee journeys it is important to first establish an agreed scope for the Employee Lifecycle within your organisation. The Employee Lifecycle Template provides you with a starting point that breaks the Employee Lifecycle into distinct stages.

At each stage you are prompted to identify the 'Moments that Matter' as these will be the most important experiences that should be prioritised for optimisation.

Lifecycle Stages	Moments that Matter						
Find Me							
Hire Me	Research	Apply	Interview	Offer / Rejection	Accept Offer	Pre-boarding	
On-board Me							
Induct Me							
Support Me							
Develop Me							
Off-board Me							
Remember Me							

JOURNEY MAP TEMPLATE

Once you have defined the Employee Lifecycle and identified the Moments that Matter, it is useful to look at a particular experience in more detail using the Journey Map Template. The template is useful to map existing journeys as well as to improve or design new ones.

To avoid journey maps becoming too complex and unwieldy, it is useful to consider a journey map in the context of a single moment and for a single employee archetype. What is the employee trying to achieve and what is the desired outcome? What touchpoints and interactions are necessary to complete the journey and how are they feeling at each step in the journey?

The Journey Map Template will also help you to identify the pain points in a journey and the opportunities to improve the employee experience.

Employee Lifecycle Stage: Hire Me		Moment that matters: Research—check out company before deciding to apply				
Employee action / outcomes	Is the role attractive and suitable?	Who is the company?	Do I know anyone there?	What is it like to work there?	Are they successful and growing?	Are they a good fit for me?
Interactions (digital, physical, human)						
Sentiment or satisfaction						
Pain Points (to be resolved)						
Opportunities (to improve)						

Sentiment / Satisfaction Icons

Love it!	Happy	Cool / nice	Meh	Surprised	Worried /nervous	Unhappy

STOP, START, CONTINUE, CHANGE CANVAS

When we are testing and reviewing new or existing journeys and experiences, it is useful to have a structured retrospective approach to obtaining feedback. The Stop, Start, Continue, Change Canvas provides that structure.

Start—what are we not doing now that would improve the experience

Stop—what is not working and should be discarded

Continue—what is working well and should be continued

Change—what should be continued but tweaked to improve its effectiveness

Employee Architype   Lifecycle Stage   Moment that Matters

STOP ■

START ▶

CONTINUE ▶▶

CHANGE ✖

For more information on the EXO Toolkit visit www.brandexperiences.com/exotoolkit

MOJO MOTIVATIONAL DASHBOARD

Mojo, powered by Motivational Maps, is the tool we have created to first understand what motivates each employee and then provide a process that can be used by managers and their teams to improve levels of motivation. We have included some sample screenshots of mojo to provide an illustration of the functionality it offers.

THE MOJO DASHBOARD SHOWING TOP 3 AND LOWEST MOTIVATORS AS WELL AS OVERALL MOTIVATION SCORE

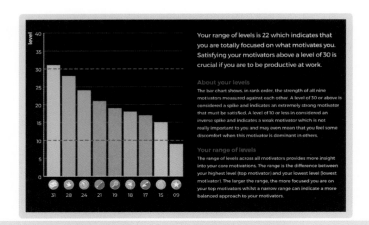

MOJO CHART SHOWING THE STRENGTH AND IMPORTANCE OF EACH MOTIVATOR TO AN INDIVIDUAL

MOJO SCORECARD SHOWING THE RELATIVE POSITION OF ALL 9 MOTIVATORS
AND CHANGES SINCE THE LAST MAP

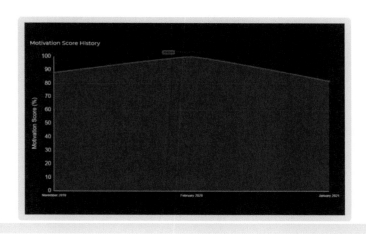

MOJO TREND ANALYSIS SHOWING THE CHANGE IN MOTIVATION LEVELS OVER TIME

MOJO TEAM DASHBOARD SHOWING TOP 3 AND LOWEST MOTIVATORS FOR A TEAM

MOJO TEAM SCORECARD SHOWING TEAM MOTIVATIONS IN ORDER OF IMPORTANCE TO THE TEAM

To find out more about mojo, please visit: www.brandexperiences.com/mojo

CONCLUSION

First of all, congratulations for reaching the end of the book!

With the content in this book and the EXO Toolkit, you should be well on the way to making a real difference to your organisation.

The real beauty of the Employee Experience Opportunity is that there are no losers—only winners:

- Your colleagues get the employee experience they deserve
- Your customers benefit from improved services, delivered by a motivated and happy workforce
- The organisation benefits from the increased productivity and revenue opportunity
- You get the funding you need to make a real and sustainable difference

Do make use of the free resources in the EXO Toolkit to provide some structure to your EX activities, and we invite you to get in touch with the us if you have any questions or would like any further help using the tools, producing your own ROI, making the business case, or anything else relating to the book.

We wish you nothing but success with your future endeavours and would love to hear about how you are using the research, knowledge and tools within your own organisations. We are always looking to improve and add value and would be delighted to receive any feedback on the book—good, bad or indifferent.

Here's to making a difference together!

Mike Sharples
www.linkedin.com/in/mikesharples

Nicholas Wardle
www.linkedin.com/in/nicholaswardle

ENDNOTES

FOOTNOTES

The Employee Experience Opportunity

1 Gallup. 'State of the Global Workplace.' Accessed 17 August 2020. https://www.gallup.com/workplace/238079/state-global-workplace-2017.aspx

Who is this book for?

2 Gallup. 'State of the Global Workplace.' Accessed 17 August 2020. https://www.gallup.com/workplace/238079/state-global-workplace-2017.aspx

3 Deloitte. 'The employee experience: Culture, engagement, and beyond.' Accessed 16 August 2020. https://www2.deloitte.com/us/en/insights/focus/human-capital-trends/2017/improving-the-employee-experience-culture-engagement.html

Introduction

4 Perkbox. 'Helping employees live better.' Accessed 16 August 2020. https://www.perkbox.com/uk/resources/library/helping-employees-live-better-in-life-and-at-work-1?m-rasn=613436.760280&xtref=www.google.com

Section One

5 wethrive. 'Future of Employee Engagement Report 2019.' Accessed 16 August 2020. https://wethrive.net/whitepaper-future-of-employee-engagement-report-2019/

6 Edelman. 'Edelman Trust Barometer 2020.' Accessed 16 August 2020. https://www.edelman.com/trustbarometer

7 Yohn, D.L. 2018. 'Fusion.' Nicholas Brealey Publishing. Boston.

8 Gallup. 'State of the Global Workplace.' Accessed 17 August 2020. https://www.gallup.com/workplace/238079/state-global-workplace-2017.aspx

Section Two

9 Gallup. 'State of the Global Workplace.' Accessed 17 August 2020. https://www.gallup.com/workplace/238079/state-global-workplace-2017.aspx

10 Deloitte. 'The employee experience: Culture, engagement, and beyond.' Accessed 16 August 2020. https://www2.deloitte.com/us/en/insights/focus/human-capital-trends/2017/improving-the-employee-experience-culture-engagement.html

11 Forbes. 'The Employee Experience Is The Future Of Work: 10 HR Trends For 2017.' Accessed 22 August 2020. https://www.forbes.com/sites/jeannemeister/2017/01/05/the-employee-experience-is-the-future-of-work-10-hr-trends-for-2017/#31843d1a20a6

12 Morgan, Jacob. 'The Employee Experience Advantage.' Wiley. 2017.

13 Willis Towers Watson. 'Breakthrough research on employee experience.' Accessed 18 August 2020. https://www.willistowerswatson.com/en-US/Insights/campaigns/breakthrough-research-on-employee-experience

14 TI People. '3... 2... 1... On the Launchpad: From strategy to Execution.' Accessed 17 August 2020. https://www.ti-people.com/state-of-ex

15 Gallup. 'Designing Your Organization's Employee Experience'. Accessed 16 August 2020. https://www.gallup.com/workplace/242252/employee-experience.aspx

16 Speakap. 'The Culture Factor: Improving Employee Loyalty and Relationships'. Accessed 17 August 2020. https://resources.speakap.com/en/culture-employee-loyalty

17 Home. 'Roundel 2020: The new Home of global employee experience trends'. Accessed 16 August 2020. https://www.thisishome.co.uk/resources/roundel-2020/

18 Gartner (Press Release). Gartner CFO Survey Reveals 74% Intend to Shift Some Employees to Remote Work Permanently. Accessed 16 August 2020. https://www.gartner.com/en/newsroom/press-releases/2020-04-03-gartner-cfo-surey-reveals-74-percent-of-organizations-to-shift-some-employees-to-remote-work-permanently2

19 Taylor, Matthew. 'Good Work: The Taylor Review of Modern Working Practices'. Accessed 16 August 2020. https://www.gov.uk/government/publications/good-work-the-taylor-review-of-modern-working-practices

20 Jacques, Elliot. Reprinted 2001. 'The Changing Culture of a Factory'. Routledge. London.

21 Yohn, D.L. 2018. 'Fusion'. Nicholas Brealey Publishing. Boston.

22 Gallup. 'State of the Global Workplace'. Accessed 17 August 2020. https://www.gallup.com/workplace/238079/state-global-workplace-2017.aspx

Section 3

23 Gallup. 'How to improve Employee Engagement'. Accessed 16 February 2021. https://www.gallup.com/workplace/285674/improve-employee-engagement-workplace.aspx

24 CIPD. 2021. 'Review of the scientific literature on Work Motivation'. Accessed 16 February 2020. https://www.cipd.co.uk/knowledge/fundamentals/relations/engagement/factsheet#gref

25 Sale, James. 'Mapping Motivation'. Routledge. 2016.

26 Lawler, E. E., & Suttle, J. L. 1973. Expectancy theory and job behavior. Organizational Behavior & Human Performance, 9(3), 482–503. https://doi.org/10.1016/0030-5073(73)90066-4

27 Gallup. 'State of the Global Workplace'. Accessed 17 August 2020. https://www.gallup.com/workplace/238079/state-global-workplace-2017.aspx

Section Six

28 Bain & Company 'The Five Disciplines of Customer Experience Leaders'. Accessed 30 August 2020. https://www.bain.com/insights/the-five-disciplines-of-customer-experience-leaders

29 Yohn, Denise Lee. Harvard Business Review. 'Why Every Company Needs a Chief Experience Officer'. Accessed 30 August 2020. https://hbr.org/2019/06/why-every-company-needs-a-chief-experience-officer

30 Corework. 'Poor Communication Leads to Project Failure One Third of the Time'. Accessed 30 August 2020. https://info.coreworx.com/blog/pmi-study-reveals-poor-communication-leads-to-project-failure-one-third-of-the-time

31 Hard, Kevin. 'Want to improve your culture? The Hard-Girling Integrated Improvement Model (IIM)'. Accessed 31 August 2020. https://www.inspiration-all.co.uk/post/10-ways-to-engage-with-your-clients

32 McKinsey & Company. 'Creating a high-performance culture'. Accessed 31 August 2020. https://www.mckinsey.com/business-functions/operations/our-insights/creating-a-high-performance-culture

INDEX

Printed in Great Britain
by Amazon

60236260R00078